How to Stop Looking for Someone Perfect and Find Someone to Love

Judith Sills, Ph.D.

How to Stop Looking for Someone Perfect and Find Someone to **LOVE**

ST. MARTIN'S PRESS ◆ NEW YORK

Design by Victoria Hartman

Library of Congress Cataloging in Publication Data
Sills, Judith.
How to stop looking for someone perfect
and find someone to love.
1. Mate selection.   I. Title.
HQ801.S583   1984   646.7'7   84-13286
ISBN 0-312-39626-0

First Edition

10 9 8 7 6 5 4 3 2 1

For My Parents,
Who Gave Me A Spectacular Head Start
and Especially For Lynn,
Who Wrote This Book With Me

Contents

viii · Contents

Acknowledgments

These are the people who helped produce this book:

Pamela Dorman, my editor . . . Susan Schulman, my agent . . . Kathy Ruggieri, first reader, typist, and general critic.

Also, my dear cousin Jane Glassman . . . Irene Schrank and Judy Gensib . . . the wonderful students in my "How to Pick a Mate" classes . . . Pamela Kerr, Patrick Buchanan, Spencer Henderson, and all those other friends, students, and patients who generously shared their life experiences and tested the ideas in this book.

Tuffy Sills Hoffman, who taught me the three rules and Lynn Hoffman, who proves my point . . . .

Finally, my mother, who makes possible everything I do.

Thank You

How to Stop Looking
for Someone Perfect
and Find Someone to Love

· 1 ·

Tell Yourself the Truth

Tell yourself the truth. You would prefer to be done with the whole dreary process of looking. You've told your story to enough strangers. You've done your marinated-steak-seduction-dinners to death. You're ready to pick a mate.

By a mate, I mean something similar to what swans and doves have. A mate is a lifetime partner. No guarantees, naturally, but what you have in mind is someone with whom you will share your decisions, your bed, your money, and your spirit; someone with whom you will have a history. Someone who will know you, in the most genuine sense.

This long-term, intimate, and highly entwined connection is certainly not the only kind of romantic link available. Everybody doesn't have to have one. It may not even end up being your most important or intense emotional link.

But it is an absolutely necessary relationship for most of us. The desire to create this kind of one-to-one continuous committed bond is so general, that 95 percent of adults marry during their lifetime.

I will sometimes use the words *marriage* and *mate* interchangeably because *marriage* symbolizes the kind of bond I am referring to. Certainly, this emotional connection can be achieved even without the trip to the altar. I am concerned with your being able to experience the spirit of a marriage, which means a true joining together. The ceremony is up to you and your mother.

I'll also use the word *single* to refer not just to legal status, but to emotional status. Single refers to anyone not currently involved as one half of a couple. You know when you're a couple. You always have to go to their family dinners and you know who you'll be with on New Year's Eve.

To Determine the Truth

The first step toward telling yourself the truth is to have a little internal conversation. When the time feels right, ask yourself this question: Would I be happier if I were sharing my life with another person?

If the word *happy* is so vague that it makes you crazy, try this: "Do I want a long-term committed relationship?" What I'm trying to get you to do is to take a serious moment, look inside, and get an answer to the question: "Do I want a mate?"

If the answer is a clear, or tentative, "no," that's not a problem. The timing may simply not be right for you. Timing is everything in these affairs, and your internal timing is crucial. Just because you are single does not mean you are, by definition, seeking a mate. Your "no" answer may mean, however, that you won't need this book *right now*.

How do you know when you *are* ready for a mate? You know you are ready when the answer to your internal question is "yes." It's as simple as that. Don't confuse yourself with all sorts of psychological doublethink that makes you wonder if the fact that you don't have a mate *means* that you don't want one. Maybe it does. But maybe it doesn't.

You probably got some sort of a yes answer to your question if you've read along this far. But "yeses" vary widely.

Yes can be a very emphatic state of mind. You'll know it is that emphatic when you tell your best friend, your father, and your chiropractor that you are looking to marry and you wonder if they know any similarly minded persons. You'll know it's that emphatic when you can't buy a new stereo because you might meet someone who already owns one.

Your answer may not be all that certain. These days it is more likely to be a wishy-washy internal dialogue that prominently features the word *if*. That's *if* as in, "I'd like a mate *if* one comes along, *if* I met the right person, *if* they are strong enough, sexy enough, smart enough, or funny enough." Or *if* as in, "*If* anyone could love me enough, stand my hours, my thighs, my family."

It doesn't matter where you are on the internal continuum between yes and maybe. You simply have to be on it somewhere. To get on it, you have to tell yourself the truth—you'd like a mate.

Most people would. You are not admitting to any peculiar deficiency in your character by seeking this kind of attachment. The reason most people want one is simple: It's better.

The best thing about marriage is, it's better than being single.

Before recently relieved divorcées and independent singles protest, let me clarify. It's better to be single than to be half of a miserable couple. But a happy mating beats being on your own any time. It's a royal flush against aces and eights.

So there's a hierarchy:

1. The Right Marriage
2. Being Single
3. The Rotten Marriage

Anyway, that's my value system. It represents the direction in which I am recommending that you steer your life, if your answer is even a weak yes. This book is a series of strategies for adding the right other person to your life. To choose that other person, you have to begin by admitting to yourself that you want one. Therefore, tell yourself the truth.

The Truth Against the Odds: The Lifted Social Eyebrow

To admit you want a mate is, for many people, an excessively difficult acknowledgment. There is definitely a stigma placed on those single people who openly acknowledge that they want to mate. The stigma makes us all talk kind of funny about it, even to ourselves.

The social stigma is applied more to women than to men. Somehow, a man who announces that he'd like to marry projects a public image of maturity, stability, and sensitivity. A woman with the same aspirations comes off sounding needy and a bit desperate. And yet, even a male will raise a few eyebrows when he says he is seeking a permanent partner, as if he's admitting a loss of interest in an active sex life. He seems weak.

Of course it's not fair. We are not concerned here with justice, we are concerned with what's true and what works. Social image affects your sense of yourself. Be judicious about where you share your personal truths. The rules for handling social scorn are:

- Always Give Yourself Good Press
- Don't Confuse the Press With the Truth

When I say "tell the truth," I don't necessarily mean tell it aloud.

Dealing with the Social Eyebrow
Rule #1: Give Yourself Good Press

"Press" usually refers to what is publicly reported in the media. This does not mean that you should be less concerned with the kind of press you get, or less concerned with your public image than the tabloids' favorite celebrity is. You are always projecting, even without elaborate media coverage, a public image of your internal thoughts and feelings. Happily, it does mean that you have more control over your image. For most of us, there is no outside reporter—we are the reporters ourselves. While you may not be the subject of nationwide attention, your feelings about yourself and long-term mating are of considerable interest to your friends, your family, and your lovers.

I am not suggesting that you lie or distort your true feelings for the sake of presenting a positive public image. Lots of people do, of course, but the psychological burden it imposes simply is not worth the juggling. No, the point is not to lie, but to be smart about yourself. Don't announce on a first date, or even on a third, that you are looking to get married. (This early announcement works best only to rid yourself of an already married sexual partner. In this situation, your desire to marry is the one unanswerable rejection.) Don't bemoan the difficulties you are having finding someone. Don't repeatedly ask colleagues at work if they have someone for you. There is nothing wrong with feeling these feelings. It just does not work for you to expose them aloud without discretion. This is an instance where it does not pay to advertise.

It does, however, pay to respond. Even without your volunteering, as a single, you will be a magnet for the question, "Do you want to get married?" This is the classic awkward inquiry for which you must be prepared with an answer, especially if the answer inside you is yes. If the answer inside you is really no, be prepared to defend or explain your rationale, but don't worry about looking weak or desperate.

The trick to answering this question is not in what you say, so much as in how much you say. If you are comfortable enough to be direct, a simple straightforward yes with no passion in your voice, followed by no explanations, ifs, or rationales, is best. Yes is a truth about yourself with which you are comfortable. "Yes, but . . ." is an indication of your anxiety. Of course you feel anxious. You don't have to expose it except where you choose to.

I am highly biased toward the direct response when used with judgment. Therefore, the simple offhand yes is an answer I favor as the best way to present yourself with integrity and still close a discussion that you didn't choose to open.

Still, I am aware that "straightforward" is simply not an interpersonal style with which many people are comfortable. Lots of you are more cautious, more tentative, less certain or simply too private to answer a question with one word. In that case, try these:

- Fall back on pet clichés such as "If the right person comes along" or "Maybe, someday, if it seemed right at the time." By clichés, I don't mean to imply that you are not telling the truth. In fact, these became clichés because they are so very true. They are a fall-back position because they reveal little about you personally.
- Try humor if you are good at it. That's humor as in "Do you want to get married?" "Well, it sure beats risking herpes," or "Well, I could use the deduction." It's not great, but it's cute and cute goes a long way to counteract "desperate" or "weak."
- If it's your style, you can go for the frontal assault. An example of the frontal assault is when a married person inquires as to how often you think of marriage and you respond, "I probably think about it as often as you think about divorce." Tone here is everything. If you can carry off whimsy, you can make it work. If not, you will sound hostile—which is easy to confuse with anxiety and desperation. You will have defeated your purpose.

Whatever you respond, I cannot recommend "I don't know" as an answer. It will probably not give you good press.

It may well be the truth, but no one believes you. Instead, it sounds like yes from someone who is afraid no one wants him.

I want to distinguish carefully between the question, "Do you want to get married?" and the intrusive assumption behind the question, "How come a nice man/woman (usually *girl*, could you gag?) like you never married?"

"Do you want to get married?" might be a genuine inquiry into the state of your thinking, but the "How come you didn't. . . ?" is a definite prejudicial judgment against your character when raised by any but the most intimate of friends. Handle it the way you would any slight.

While it's one thing when family and friends ask you about marriage, it is a much different issue when this question is posed by a potential mate. He or she is asking out of a vested interest. Therefore, the question and its timing has something to do with the relationship between the two of you.

The general folk wisdom for handling the situation is to lie—that is, not to admit your real intentions for fear of scaring off your potential partner.

I subscribe to this stance up to a point. As a rule of thumb, don't spend over six months in an intimate relationship without sharing the fact that it is your intention to marry during your lifetime. You may or may not be admitting to a desire to marry the person asking the question. But it is fair all around, and in your own best interests, to be clear about your goals with those closest to you.

If you don't feel safe enough with, or close enough to your romantic partner to share such an important aspiration, what have you been doing for six months?

Rule #2: Don't Confuse Your Press with the Truth

Remember, the purpose of all this is to overcome the obstacles that stand in the way of telling yourself the truth. Learning how to minimize social scorn by presenting a smoother, more relaxed social image is meant to make you more comfortable with the truth.

"Press" is just that—a hype, an image, a shell. It is what is perceived about you but *it is not you.* The ability to keep these things separate and juggle both develops over time and with a good deal of self-awareness.

The major risk of creating a public image, whether for seeking a mate or any other endeavor, is that you may become more familiar with the image than with your real thoughts and feelings. You begin to believe your own notices. You lose touch with your interior. You start to know only as much about yourself as someone meeting you for the first time.

In highly technical psychological jargon, we call the people who confuse their press with the truth phonies. A phony is a person so concerned with projecting a public image that one is uncertain there is anyone at all inside.

I am warning you about the dangerous extremes. When I say "be conscious of your own press," I mean specifically with respect to overcoming the social squinting so often directed toward single people. When I say "don't confuse your press with the truth," I mean, don't confuse the need to *downplay* your loneliness and dissatisfaction with the ability to acknowledge to yourself that the loneliness and dissatisfaction are there.

After all, if not for this loneliness and dissatisfaction, what would propel you through all of the ordeals of courtship? You need to acknowledge these feelings to yourself. You just don't need to advertise them.

The other big advantage to deliberately projecting a positive image is that it can work to soothe some of your fears. Sometimes the simple act of saying aloud that you are confident of finding a mate can also make you *feel* more confident.

This is what we are working toward. If the first step in

choosing a mate is admitting to yourself that you want one, ideally that admission won't be a panicked, frenzied plea. There is no reason to panic. If you want a mate, and you are clear and realistic about what you want, you'll get one.

The Truth Against the Odds: Independence

Was there ever a value system guilty of more overkill than the done-to-death theme of the Joys of Independence? In the 1970s, this was the poster philosophy whose Magna Carta was: "You go your way and I'll go mine and if our paths should cross, well, I'll buy you a drink . . ."—or words to that effect.

Ironically, this same philosophy also fervently espoused the joys of the multiple orgasm, although how one could be so damned independent and so utterly sexually fulfilled always seemed a problem to me. Every time he went his way and I went mine, we both went home alone.

I don't mean to dismiss the importance of the philosophy of independence. I just want to put it in perspective. In fact, people who are independent enough to take care of themselves do make better mates.

What I am concerned about is the confusion in thinking that allowed *independent* to mean *alone.* Follow this line of thinking and the desire to connect with another person becomes a weakness, an acknowledgment to yourself that you are needy.

Nobody wants to see him or herself as "needy." The effect of an emphasis on independence can be a reluctance to tell the truth even to oneself about how much you need to be connected to another. You may be forced to look for a mate behind your own back.

Looking for a Mate Behind Your Own Back

When the direct pursuit of a goal causes a lot of anxiety,

you may be sometimes forced to sneak off quietly so as to avoid disapproval.

Perhaps you did this as a kid, when you snuck off for a beer or a cigarette, because you knew you'd be in big trouble if you did it openly. You wanted the experience, but not the punishment, so you did it behind your parents' backs.

Maybe you've had a period when your romantic choices didn't exactly move your parents or friends to applause. Perhaps there was someone to whom you were attracted, but whose presence in your social world was a source of discomfort to you. This is often the case when people consider your partner of the wrong social class, age, religion, or appearance. A lot of people use sneaking as a coping strategy in these uncomfortable situations. They do what they want to do, but they do it privately. It's a carefully guarded secret.

But what if *you* are the one who disapproves or gets anxious? You're uncomfortable with your self-image when you're honest about what you want. The desire to mate, especially given all the social pressure about the satisfactions of being alone, can present this kind of dilemma.

If you learn as a child, and we all do, that sneaking is a workable way to do what you want and still avoid disapproval, it's natural to act that way even with yourself.

You know what you end up doing? You end up being a sneak. Behind your own back. Specifically:

1. You feel an urge to mate but,
2. You see yourself as an independent, self-sufficient person who,
3. Views mating as something to do "if it comes along" so,
4. You can't actively seek to find someone, because your kind of person doesn't need to do that, therefore,
5. You look indirectly, half consciously, without focusing clearly on your goal, without really acknowledging your purpose. In other words:
6. *You look for a mate behind your own back.*

Fear of violating the social value of autonomy is only one major motivation for looking behind your own back. The second is *superstition.*

A most formidable obstacle to telling yourself the truth is the superstition that only those people who don't want a mate, who are essentially busy doing other things, will find one.

There is a useful purpose to this folk wisdom: It is a way of advising people to relax about their feelings. It revolves around the idea we discussed earlier that no one wants to present a public image of weakness or desperation. But sitting on your hands doesn't help you reach your goal and find a mate.

It's another example of a good idea getting distorted. To the extent that this folklore works to help you relax and enjoy life through whichever of its stages you happen to be living, it's terrific. Nonetheless, when it's taken literally, it urges people to deny what they are seeking in the magical hope that it will suddenly appear. Again, it forces you to look for one of life's biggest rewards *behind your own back.* And if you cannot acknowledge that you are seeking something, *how do you know when you've found it?*

The Truth Against the Odds: Past Failure

The hardest obstacle to overcome, when you are seeking to tell the truth, is the barrier built by past pain.

Clearly this does not apply to everyone. In fact, if you are under twenty-five or so, you may not have to struggle with this obstacle at all. I don't mean to suggest that people under twenty-five have no experience of pain. Actually, anyone that close to adolescence is probably still reeling.

It's just that singles (remember, I mean widowed, divorced, or never married) over the age of twenty-five must often cope with the long-term scars left by painful romantic experiences. These are the psychological scars that can make the renewed interest in mating an anxious, unpleasant, even frightening feeling. Fear can make it difficult to tell yourself the truth.

If you've never married, and you've wanted to, you are likely to be suffering to some degree from the scars of repeated disappointment. After a series of connections that somehow fail to come to fruition, people often feel a sense of personal failure, that whatever went wrong is *their fault*.

And often, their response is to withdraw. They give up the attempt, retreating to their apartments, spending time in the safe world of close friends, diving into their work. They give up because the whole courtship ritual is too painful, too humiliating, too frustrating.

The emotional holocaust of divorce can easily precipitate this kind of withdrawal. Divorce is so common that people are often taken aback at the degree of emotional devastation it wreaks. There is a widespread supposition that if so many people go through it, it can't be all that awful.

For a lot of people, it is. It can be an utterly life-crumbling upheaval of loss, despair, and misery that continues for a shockingly long period of time. Nonetheless, many people *do* live through this lousy period in life, put the pieces back in place, and get on with their lives.

Divorced people are often left with a residual fear that hampers their ability to look for a new mate. Like car accident victims who become car phobic for a while, divorced people know that it *can* happen to them. The horror of ever having to endure another divorce is a hell of an obstacle to telling yourself that you'd like to remarry.

Whether single or divorced, it's scary to think that you will repeat your past mistakes and doom yourself to recapitulate past misery. You know you are wiser—but still you. The inevitable bad solution that many people test out for a while is to caricature their former relationship and seek out:

• the complete opposite, or

- someone with all of their ex's good points and none of the bad, forgetting that new people will have flaws all of their own, or,
- a series of safe relationships that provide companionship, but not intimacy, thereby avoiding the risk of a second emotional upheaval.

All singles would like to avoid repeating past mistakes in relationships, but they aren't clear how to go about it. It makes it hard for them to tell themselves the truth. What they need very badly is a model for choosing a mate. They need to learn how to look.

Learning How to Look

The fairy tale goes like this: "A mate is someone who comes along while you are busy doing other things." There you are, studying for finals, nary a thought about the future in your serious-minded little head and along comes the prettiest girl in the library. You make her laugh. Three dates later you make her come. Three years later you have your first child. Thirty years later, her breasts are still perky and she's still laughing at your jokes.

Or, you are thirty-three, respectably if not fascinatingly employed. You haven't formally dated in two years and neither has anyone else you know. Your love affairs are with friendly acquaintances. They don't expect much and neither do you. One day you walk into a meeting and catch the eye of an attractive account executive. You lunch. You agree to a movie for Friday evening. It goes so well that he is still there on Monday. Happily, you find that you are in love. Luckily, you find that you are suited. You mate. The End.

I would never mean to suggest that these situations don't occur. They do. I simply think that relying on them for your happiness is haphazard, inefficient, and unnecessary.

I would even go one step further. Those individuals who

are actively seeking a mate *and* who have a clear idea about the sort of person who would satisfy them, have a significantly better shot at choosing the right person. Clear thinking, focused attention, and realistic goals are just better bets than crossed fingers and "magic."

I think lots of you would agree, if you felt able to make that sort of realistic appraisal of yourself and a potential mate. It's not that difficult to do. You just have to learn how to look, and that is the purpose of this book.

Overcoming Your Attitude

Now we've never met, but if you have anything in common with the single people with whom I have worked, I know we have one major obstacle to overcome. It's called "Negative Attitude."

The symptoms of negative attitude are unmistakable. You are a victim of negative attitude if you hold privately, or more likely, share openly, any of the following opinions:

1. "There are no strong men."

This theme can be expanded at length. It centers around the angry and disappointed observation that men are children, really wanting a mother, not a wife, are frightened, intimidated, or otherwise put off by "strong women." They require all sorts of care and nurturing for their egos but are unwilling or unable to return the favor. In general, you say, they are more trouble than they are worth.

Corollaries to this attitude include the opinion that every man you meet is:

- hopelessly disorganized, incompetent at handling domestic responsibility, and literally unable to dress himself if you don't pre-match his socks with his shirt, or
- excessively rigid, with a life full of rules for demand feeding and demand freedom that must be catered to

with infantile regularity, leaving little or no room for your own needs.

2. "Women are so pushy."

This conviction centers around the heartfelt complaint that women's expectations about you, your work, your success, your choice of food, friends, and footwear are endless and impossible. She says she's looking for love but what she really wants is a meal ticket and an eventual mink. She says it's you she loves, but the minute you reciprocate, she dives in and starts to change you. She thinks you should ask for a raise, quit drinking, and drop your loud friend Harry. She thinks the old couch won't do and neither will your income. She calls it a woman's touch, but you recognize it as an act of aggression.

3. "Men are all afraid of commitment."

This is the one where you say to yourself: "I mean, what's the point?" They love to have you there to sleep with and to do the cleaning up. They appreciate a sympathetic ear and they are not loath to enjoy your cooking. Many are even free with a lot of "I love you's" and "you're terrific's." But when you start thinking of children and shared bank accounts, they make speeches that begin with the word *freedom* and end in a red-faced mumble of ". . . not ready . . ." Extensions of this universal complaint include:

- men don't talk about their feelings
- men are too insecure to be faithful
- men hate change

4. "Women are so hypocritical."

You can't trust them, they aren't reasonable. They aren't willing to compromise. They want to be equal to men but they want to be treated like women. They want you to earn the serious living, while they make the "extra" money. They only want to talk about feelings, but they could kill when you call them emotional. They stoop low to win an argument. They cry and carry on. But if you get angry, they accuse you of refusing to talk or of trying to intimidate them.

Most complaints of singles fall into these categories, although they may be expressed more generally: "They're all a bunch of losers," "They're all so self-centered," "They're all scared to death," "They are only looking to get laid," "They are only looking to get married," and on and on and on. . . . Do you recognize any of these attitudes in yourself? To the extent that you do, you are suffering from negative attitude and it is a serious obstacle to choosing a mate.

To take the first step toward freeing yourself of this barrier, you must recognize these attitudes for what they are: They are your perceptions of the world, personal visions of the world—they are not the world itself.

We all have a way of interpreting or understanding what we see. Then we gather more information, interpret it through our expectations, and *voilà*! it confirms our original impression.

No, you're not crazy. To a great extent these universal complaints exist because they *are* common experiences for a lot of men and a lot of women. It is absolutely true that, as filtered through the fantasies and expectations of most women, men are often weak. Conversely, if examined through the unrealistic and uncomprehending eyes of men, women are shallow and hypocritical.

It's not that these judgments are totally erroneous. But how much better off is your life if you allow yourself to make these judgments?

If you sum up all the complaints of singles who are looking over the field and denigrating potential partners, you come back to one universal plaint. Henry Higgins sang about it when he whined, "Why can't a woman be more like a man?"

♣

If you're a single woman, you might have joked about it when you wished for a mate you'd get along with as well as you do with your best girlfriend.

Face it: If you are heterosexual, you are seeking a mate from a member of an alien tribe. Their folkways are different; their rites and rituals can be silly or appalling. You have two ways to go in this situation:

- You can play the anthropologist and develop an appreciation of the cultural differences, cultivating a loving sense of humor to get you over the wider chasms, or
- You can play the commando and seek a mate among the enemy.

There's a problem with turning the opposite sex into the enemy. You will always harbor anxiety about when they'll try to get you. What is really a difference in world view will be experienced as a personal assault. What might be viewed as differing expectations will get labeled as matters of right and wrong. You will be a victim of your own negative attitudes.

If you cannot get past negative attitudes, you won't be looking for a mate. You'll be looking to prove that no one out there is worthy.

For all of you who are waiting until the "right person comes along," negative attitude may have cost you the difference between knowing Mr. or Ms. Right and waiting for Mr. or Ms. Perfect.

Maybe you read over this section and, seeing these extremes in black and white, you refused to believe that *you* hold such extreme opinions. Whenever one prints the extremes, they are always patently silly and easy to reject. Still, I must ask you—have you listened, really listened to yourself lately?

I've been listening to single people for a long time and I hear the kind of complaints I've described over and over again. Well, you might admit to having uttered them, but you would argue it was just a figure of speech, a turn of phrase, or a moment of frustration. Of course you know that all men aren't one way and all women aren't another. Still, those casual, negative generalizations affect you more than you may realize.

A Lecture

You walk into a party or a bar and in three minutes (more likely three seconds, but I'm giving you the benefit of the doubt) you've made a judgment: There's no one here who's my type. They're all jerks. You may even pride yourself on knowing your tastes and preferences so well that you seldom err in your first impressions of potential mates.

I would like to focus your attention on two points. First, if you are a person who takes pride in these lightning-quick judgments of others, I'll bet that you find your judgments are predominantly negative. People who allow themselves to make rapid judgments most often make negative ones because they're very safe. If you avoid someone because, in your opinion, he's a fool or she's flaky, how can you ever really be proved wrong? You can simply chalk it up to matters of taste, pride yourself on your pickiness, and avoid that person so you never have an opportunity to discover if you're wrong.

Positive attitudes and positive judgments are riskier. They open you up to more people, more experiences, and the possibility of disappointment. Of course, they open you up to the possibility of more happiness as well, but many people cling hard to the better-safe-than-sorry stance.

Please forgive this lecture. It's just that it has sometimes been so frustrating for me to listen to people who are genuinely lonely react critically to a potential partner because of the most trivial idiosyncrasies and on the most premature of opinions. Most men and women report to me that they judge whether or not someone could ever be a potential partner at first glance. These same people would report that physical appearance is only one, and not the most important one, of many criteria for choosing a mate. Then why screen out so many potential candidates at first sight?

I hear lonely people reject possibilities because "His teeth are capped" or "She's too short" or "He wore white socks" or "She watches too much television." It is very difficult to move people who are stuck in such trivia. They will agree *theoretically* that it's unimportant, but they experience themselves as the victims of their internal feelings. They say "*It turned me off*" as if one is utterly without control of one's emotions.

This is the most negative attitude of them all: the perspective that *someone else* must push all the right buttons and your response is entirely out of your control. Of course, anyone who is so helpless before his or her own negative attitudes has only one option—to wait for magic. The catch is, it can be a very long wait and the magic can be a very short ride.

End of lecture.

I do understand that your complaints are not entirely based on negative attitudes—they are an expression of your frustration, your disappointment. Some of you feel you've been looking forever and have nothing to show for it. Naturally, you put the blame on what's out there.

I think the problem is less with what's out there than with how you've learned to look. Your frustration is the result of having a set of expectations that isn't being met. Perhaps the problem lies with expectations themselves.

The Wish List

I'll bet you have one. It's your little (or long, God forbid) mental checklist. You carry a mental picture of Mr. or Ms. Perfect and you're quickly able to evaluate a potential mate according to the list.

You can figure out your own wish list rather quickly if you'll take a moment. Just complete this exercise:

When I picture my mate, s/he would ideally be:

1.	6.
2.	7.
3.	8
4.	9.
5.	10.

Here are examples of some other people's wish lists.

Kathy, 26, never married, but confident of a future relationship:

1. attractive	6. experienced
2. sense of humor	7. sensitive, affectionate
3. energetic	8. family-oriented
4. successful	9. calm
5. older than I am	10.

Kathy paused here for one moment, reviewing her list. Then she laughed and added, "You know, Dr. Sills, it's all of those things that everyone says they want and no one ever finds. . . ."

Greg, 31, a commercial artist, recently fallen in love and hoping for the best. She'd be:

1. professional, independent—I mean involved in her own career

2. attractive

3. older than I am (This is a recent addition to Greg's list, reflecting the unexpected pleasures of his new relationship with a slightly older woman.)

4. a creative thinker
5. outgoing/socially at ease
6. somewhere between earth mother and sophisticated
7. not a flashy dresser—in fact, understated in every way
8. a woman who can take care of herself

By comparison, here is Elizabeth's wish list. She is the 62-year-old divorcee after a 28-year-long marriage. He would:

1. put me on a pedestal—want to devote himself to caring for me
2. want to protect me from money, business, all the harsh realities. He would really cherish me.
3. be in his sixties
4. be well turned-out, well groomed—no polyester!
5. have good taste—appreciate the finer things
6. know his way around the world
7. I want someone who is adventurous—not staid—someone whose attitude is "I'm only going to live once, I want to do it all. . . ."

Last, take a look at Sam's list. He's a 43-year-old self-employed businessman, divorced and something of a success with the ladies. Sam's ideal is simple. She'll have:

1. great legs
2. a great brain
3. She won't be "too much of a lady."

You know what the wish list really is? It's a partial inventory of your expectations. Although you understand that your wish list is merely a set of ideal traits, it has a powerful influence on how you look *and* who you overlook.

So your wish list can become your list of expectations. What's wrong with having expectations?

Well, on the face of it, nothing.

Expectations are natural, normal, and necessary. I am not a subscriber to the school that suggests you should expect nothing from anybody and so avoid disappointment; that's another case of "better safe than sorry." My preferred cliché is: Nothing ventured, nothing gained. Besides, it's utterly impractical to think that two people could interact smoothly on a day-to-day basis without some clearly expected behaviors occurring to provide stability and continuity.

You didn't just swoop into this bar, this party, this relationship from outer space. You have a past, a family, a culture, an education. Out of all these experiences has evolved a set of expectations about what a mate might offer you, and how he or she might be expected to behave. How could you possibly choose a mate without a set of personal expectations about how he or she should be?

It's not having expectations that's a problem, it's some of the expectations themselves.

The One-Size-Fits-All Fallacy

Take another look at those wish lists. In the end, they are all pretty much describing the same person. Oh, the ages vary, and there are shades of difference in personal styles, but on the whole, the wish inventory is a general one.

One gets the feeling that everyone is looking for the same person. *He* has to be respectably, professionally employed (at least compared to you), must be at least minimally "cute," be able to strike you as intelligent, and have a sense of humor. Most of all, he must give the impression that he will take better care of you than you can of yourself.

She has to be physically attractive or rich, at least compared to you. She doesn't have to be both, but she does need to be at the desirable extreme of one of these. She must be capable of loyalty and understanding and be just as sexy as you are comfortable with . . . a bit less perhaps, but never more. . . .

This is the one-size-fits-all fallacy. Your set of expectations looks like everybody else's. It may have little to do with what you need to give you a shot at a satisfying relationship. Yet you allow these expectations to color your appreciation of potential mates.

Understanding what you need as opposed to what your friends need or what everyone who is interested thinks you need is the key to making a wise choice of a mate.

You must begin to differentiate yourself from the group so that your expectations can reflect you.

There are three questions you can ask to help you examine your expectations.

1. *Are these expectations yours or your parents'?*
This may be self-evident, but it's still worth a moment's pause. The expectations of your family about your future mate are as institutionalized as mother-in-law jokes. Your family has a myriad of subtle and direct ways of letting you know what they want. (I remember my mother putting me off an infatuation with one swift sentence. "He's nice enough, dear, but don't you think he's a bit odd?" He never looked quite right to me again.)

Certainly your family is entitled to some distinct opinions about who would be suitable for you. In fact, they know you well and have a chance of being right, but keep in mind that they have at least an equal chance of being wrong.

You've picked up a lot of assumptions from your family about the necessary characteristics of a prospective partner. You may agree with all of them or they may be entirely inappropriate. The point is: Your family's expectations require a personal internal review. Too often, we're on automatic pilot when it comes to relationships—set for someone else's course.

2. *Are these expectations left over from an earlier time in your life?*
The stereotypes about mating can be so powerful that

while you change, your wish list might remain frozen in time.

Each era in your life brings with it a different set of needs that must be filled by other people. Generally speaking, the total set of expectations doesn't change all that much. Physical appeal, though it may have shifted from "cute" to "distinguished," still figures prominently, as does temperament, employment, and commitment. But the priorities you have vis-à-vis these characteristics may have changed. Where you were concerned with passion at twenty, you may prefer security at forty. Where her career might have been a matter of indifference when you were twenty-five, it may be a requirement at forty-five.

These shifts in priorities can be a special problem for those of you who are looking for the second time around after disappearing from the singles' world for some significant era in your life. You haven't had much time to rethink your needs. Unless you make the time, setting aside a serious period of self-examination, you are likely to rely on the same wish list you used fifteen years ago.

3. *Are you succumbing to social pressure?*

Don't please the world, please yourself. If you're only pleased with yourself when the world approves of you, you have a problem in choosing a mate.

The problem is that your social group has a very clear status ranking of desirable mates. There are all sorts of rules about which age range, physical qualities, occupations, or life-styles are appropriate for you. These rules are made for society as a whole. They may or may not be of value to you. You will need to call each of these into question if you want your expectations to reflect what you genuinely need instead of what you were taught to expect.

To the extent that you can differentiate yourself from your parents, your friends, or your own childhood, you will not fall victim to the One-Size-Fits-All Fallacy. You will really be learning how to look.

Let's say your wish list is up-to-date. Further, suppose you re-examine your expectations and they seem reasonable to you. Even with a perfectly revised wish list, a really individually tailored set of expectations, you're not home free. To learn how to look, you need to learn to use your list. Your expectations should not be carved in stone.

The Ten Commandments Syndrome

Here's the awful truth. Nobody is going to live up to your expectations. You'll tell me that you know that, but do you? If you really understand that nobody is going to live up to your expectations, why do you have such a morbid fear of "settling"?

Your Aunt Frances says to you, "Gloria, don't be so fussy," and you assume she's advising you to settle. There will be times in this book when you think I'm giving you the same advice.

"Settle" here means "settle for less than you want, just to be married." It implies that if you have enough to offer, you'll get someone up to your standards, while lesser people will have to settle to get anyone at all.

Fear of Settling is a sign that you're taking your expectations way too seriously. If you know that nobody can meet all of your expectations, what's so terrible about hooking up with someone who doesn't?

Your wish list is only a set of preferences or assumptions about how a partner might be. It's not written in stone. It's not some measure of what you deserve. It's simply a comment on what you prefer to anticipate.

Yet when someone does not measure up on your list, you are left with a dreadful uncertainty. You feel you've lowered yourself, or you worry that people will think you have. You are a victim of the Ten Commandments Syndrome.

The Ten Commandments Syndrome sufferer confuses settling with compromise.

Isn't compromise an odd word? On the one hand it means

"a result of a settlement reached by mutual consent." What a lovely idea and, everyone would agree, what a necessary ingredient in an intimate relationship. But when you confuse "compromise" with "settling," you get a whole different feeling. "Settling" implies defeat and resentment: You lost. In a good compromise, everybody wins.

If you want to find a mate, the single best thing you can do is trade your fear of settling for a willingness to compromise. After all, being able to compromise may be on someone else's list of expectations you'll have to fulfill.

There's another advantage to trading in your tablet for a set of expectations taken lightly. As I discussed earlier, not all your expectations are positive. Each of those complaints of singles can develop into secret expectations. In the end, you come to expect that the new man in your life will be afraid of commitment or that every woman you meet will be too demanding.

You are developing a set of self-fulfilling prophecies. Just remember, someone looking for a fight is more likely to find one—same thing with someone looking for disappointment.

The only way to pick the right mate is to get past your complaints, your rules, and your disappointments. In order to decide which relationships are worth pursuing you need one thing: You need to learn how to look.

Don't feel as though you should have learned this already. We don't help people much with this sort of thing. You are thrown back on the self-interested advice of your friends, the anxious observations of your mother and the dubious reliability of your hormones.

In fact, you get more instruction about how to buy a car or a washing machine than about how to pick a mate. No one would suggest you choose a car simply because it gives you a warm, creamy feeling when you look at it, although that's a better reason to choose a car than a mate—the trade-ins are so much less painful. You are expected to make a rational decision that balances personal appeal with practicality. It makes sense to you to do this. You seek advice, figure out your needs, and choose.

You can learn to look for a mate in the same rational manner. All that is required is that you:

- clarify for yourself what it is that you are looking for
- learn to recognize what someone else has to offer

How to Stop Looking for Someone Perfect and Find Someone to Love is a guide to these two tasks.

·2·

Three Golden Rules

Go ahead, snicker. You've assumed that mating was a matter of destiny and circumstance; a matter of the heart, not a subject for *Consumer Reports*.

Not necessarily. At least your aunt had some idea that it was also a matter of exposure. ("Go ahead, maybe he'll have a friend . . ."); and your grandmother had an idea that it was a matter of clarity of purpose ("Marry in haste and repent at leisure."); or you yourself acknowledge that there are some predictable aspects of development. ("Meet her mother. You'll see what she'll be like in twenty years.")

Still, the whole process is anxious and confusing. One way to deal with the anxiety is to close the whole question and swathe it in the mystique of romance. ("When you meet the right person, darling, you'll know.")

Another way to handle the confusion is to elevate it. What is really confusion gets labeled as chemistry, and chemistry gets labeled as love, and love is far too tender to subject to the rigors of rational analysis.

All of this is fine if it's working for you. You can tell if it's working for you if you are satisfactorily coupled or blessedly, relievedly single.

Let's say you're not. If you're not, there's nothing odd or even unique about you. Human beings have a strong natural desire for intimacy and most of them satisfy the bulk of that desire through the selection of a single, special partner. In the absence of that, you are likely to feel unfinished or unconnected.

If that describes you, either because you have never mated or it didn't work out the first time and you have re-entered the selection process, you might want to reconsider all those assumptions about destiny and true love.

There is a way to think more rationally about how to pick a mate. It doesn't ignore love or luck, but it doesn't leave you at their mercy either.

To begin with, there are three golden rules, three guiding principles you can use to help clarify your thinking when you have come to the point of thinking about mating.

If you read no further in this book, these three rules will still be invaluable to you. They are designed to help you think about the central issues in a very complicated decision.

Yes, you can think, even while you feel. What happens too often is that, especially where love and sex are concerned, we feel, then we act. It becomes very difficult to shape these actions through the mediating process of rational thought. The thing is, thinking can help.

Even people who agree with this, encounter a big obstacle in doing it. The obstacle is: They don't know *what to think about.*

If you make the assumption that mating is essentially an emotional process, you end up thinking mostly about how you feel. This can result in an endless merry-go-round of emotional temperature-taking, ending up pretty much where you started.

The purpose of these three central rules, then, is *to give you something to think about.* The thinking part of you is not necessarily the best or most important part of you, but it sure can be an ally when you want to plan a strategy or make a decision.

In addition to something to think about, the purpose of these rules is to help you *keep thinking* when emotion threatens to overwhelm you. It is easy to get swamped with feeling when you are in the process of mating. God knows, sexual arousal alone can make the brightest among us absolute sapheads. Mix in a little loneliness, a fair share of hope, a history of disappointment, and a healthy dose of social pressure and you've got all the ingredients for the emotional morass that so often accompanies courtship.

It's no wonder that so many people give up. The whole thing can feel impossible to control, plus it hurts a lot. Please don't give up. It's a wonderful thing to share your life, and the process of finding someone to do it with doesn't have to be a stab in the dark or a stab in the back.

You can start over again, this time armed with the three cardinal rules.

Okay, let's get going. What do you think is the single most important characteristic someone must have to qualify as your mate? Take the position that you are screening potential candidates. (You probably always are, of course, though you might not allow yourself to think it out loud.) At a first meeting, what single attribute must potential candidates have before you go one step further in a relationship with them?

Rule #1: Availability

The single most important feature of a relationship that you hope will develop into marriage, is that the candidate be *available* for marriage.

You cannot get around this. It does not matter how instantly you are attracted to his body or her bank account, or how immediately emotionally drawn you are to one another. If the other person is unavailable, for any of several reasons, he or she will not become your mate.

Availability is not as straightforward as it seems. No one is completely closed to redesigning a life around a new person. Nor is anyone totally prepared to greet that kind of change with open arms.

However, when you are picking a mate, you are playing the odds. Nobody bets a horse that isn't even in the race. When you check for availability, there's no question that some people are very much in the race. You are better off going with them.

There are two kinds of availability to consider when evaluating a potential mate: situational and psychological. Both are important.

Situational availability refers to a person's relationship status. You know, nature abhors a vacuum, but two's company, three's a crowd. Someone who already has a mate is not a good candidate for you.

Sounds obvious, doesn't it? Then how come so many of you are investing so much time in a relationship with someone who is already taken? (I know, because there's nobody else, because it's true love, because it's so great in bed. . . . Think it over.)

Think of situational availability on a continuum from the least available to become your mate to the most. Least available is someone who is already married, especially where that marriage has already produced children. I'm not suggesting that the person will never get a divorce. In fact, close to one out of two of those people do. And it's likely that that person will pick a new mate (85 percent of divorced men and 75 percent of divorced women remarry). It's just that, at this point in their lives, these people are unavailable to you. You must learn to take people where you find them. If you find them in a marriage, the chances are very low that they will end up marrying you.

Next, consider that group of people whose external status is technically single, but who have strong emotional and situational ties to another person. On a scale from the least available to the most available, this would include:

1. Someone in a long-term living arrangement with a mate.

The absence of marriage could be the reflection of a life philosophy, a lack of commitment, some unresolved problem in the relationship, or a legal/financial situation that precludes marriage. When you are screening potential candidates, you are not likely to know the reason that their live-in lover is not their spouse. It doesn't matter. People who live with their lovers are unlikely to be available to be your mate.

2. Someone who is separated.

We're getting better here, but still in the danger zone. The danger is twofold. First, separated from a marriage is still legally married. So keep reminding yourself that a person married to someone else is not available to marry you.

Second, the person who is separated is in a process of disengaging emotional threads from another situation. He or she may, and often does, long for a warm body in a suddenly empty bed or a comforting face to play out all of the positive sides of coupling—the planning, the shared jokes, the human presence. I'm not suggesting that a separated person might not be available for a new relationship. They are often not available for a new marriage and are not likely candidates to be your mate.

3. Someone who is divorced.

Ah, we're getting into the group of real possibilities. Depending. A divorced person is available to be your mate depending on:

• How long s/he has been divorced (the median remarriage time is forty-four months after divorce).

• Financial issues.

Divorced people have usually abruptly altered their financial circumstances. They may be bearing the long-term financial responsibilities of a previous relationship, in the form of alimony or child support. They may be in a suddenly straitened situation because they are now the sole support of a family that was built on two incomes.

When these people enter new relationships, financial need, financial arrangements, and financial responsibilities are more significant issues for them than for people who have never been in this situation.

Money is always a tense subject, particularly where love is concerned. You will, however, need to pay special attention to these issues as you evaluate a divorced person's availability to you, *and* when you consider your availability to them. When you mate, it is customary to assume each other's financial responsibilities. The readiness or reluctance of the divorced person to be re-involved in a financial relationship will be a significant issue in evaluating his or her availability.

• Kids.

A striking difference between divorced people and singles is the appendage many divorcees have developed known as children. You might as well look at it as if they've grown another limb, because these children are as much a part of this candidate's life as a body part. You are, therefore, no longer simply picking a mate, you are picking a family.

This is true even if the kids are not currently in the picture much. Perhaps they are living with the ex-spouse. Marriage is a long-term proposition. Where child care is concerned, responsibilities often shift between divorced parents over the years.

It is easy to begin a relationship with someone whose family forms a shadowy background, particularly if that person doesn't have full-time custody of the kids. When you are as caught up as your partner is in the mystique of a new relationship, you may have to force your attention to the hidden agenda: Am I available to be a co-parent? Or conversely: Do I want to bring a new family member into my children's life?

I mention these relatively obvious facts only to focus your attention on your response to them. For many, a new family is not an obstacle, but an asset. If you are divorced and raising children, a new family member in the role of step-parent might be a blessing. A lot depends on who the children are and what they are like.

• Psychological availability for remarriage. We'll discuss this in the next section of this chapter.

4. *Someone who is single but whose situation includes strong emotional and/or financial ties that preclude marriage to you.*

The bulk of this category includes two sets of people: those with heavy nuclear family responsibilities and those who have married their work.

The man or woman with a long history of difficulty separating from his or her family of origin is giving you an indirect message that he or she is probably not available to start a new family with you. Some clues to this attachment might be people over thirty who have never lived away from their parents or people who are responsible for the direct care of invalid parents or younger siblings.

A job involvement can mirror this family attachment. That involvement might be with the career itself. For example, the medical student might focus all of his or her attention on time-consuming professional development for the seven to ten years of training before practice.

The involvement might be with some significant person at the job who comes to substitute for a mate in this person's life. The "office wife" is a classic example of the person in this situation. She is often in a responsible, interesting position that requires many hours and intense commitment. (Think of American presidents and their career-long, dedicated secretaries.)

Developing an intimate relationship takes a considerable investment of time. To be genuinely available for such a relationship, one must make available, as a priority, the time required. When time is already substantially invested elsewhere, that is usually an indication that emotions are invested elsewhere too.

The optimistic side in this category is that often people with substantial investments elsewhere reach a point where they are ready to become available to a mate. Sometimes the external circumstances change. The aging parent dies, the professional completes training. A shift in one's life situation often brings about a shift in attitude, a new set of needs.

Sometimes with no alteration in circumstance, a person reaches a new developmental point. Then, what was satisfying or felt as an obligation, no longer is. He or she begins to look around for something new. At this point, the person becomes available.

Of course, it's difficult to do a really thorough screening around these issues. You are dealing with someone who is available in the traditional sense (there is no mate) but whose history indicates that he or she has not really been available and might not be to you. It's not always obvious, even to the person in question, when needs shift and availability changes. It will be hard for you to evaluate.

Investment of time is a good rule of thumb to help you assess the availability of people in this situation. Someone who wants a relationship with you makes time for it. To some degree, the amount of time people make available will be a measure of how much intimacy they are seeking. You simply cannot get very close to someone you only date on Saturday night.

Speaking of dating, the third group of people who would logically fall in this category are people who are dating, "going with," or otherwise emotionally tied to a potential mate. Lots of people are involved with someone else, in some fashion, when you meet them. If they have not merged their lives, at least to the point of informally living together, or having an "understanding" or an informal engagement, you can consider them single and available.

Nonetheless, you will want to assess the nature of this dating relationship to get a clear picture of how entangled your candidate is. Once again, time can be your rule of thumb. People do pretty much what they want to do. "Want" here means where the feelings lie, where the emotional impulse is. If someone is making a significant amount of time available to you, you can feel more comfortable about his or her lack of involvement elsewhere.

Maybe, you say. But what if he's carrying a torch? What if she is spending time with you because the other person is unavailable to her? Then you are dealing with someone who is in the category of those separated but not yet divorced. This is true even though the divorce here refers to a psychological one and not a legal one. All the same restrictions on availability apply.

5. *People for whom sexual preference is an issue.*

There is a whole group of people who might make strong, rewarding lifelong companions but for the obstacle of their own sexual ambivalence. I am not speaking here about people who are clear that their choice of a mate should be a same-sex partner, because that is their clear sexual preference. For people who are seeking a same-sex partner, the strategies for picking a mate suggested in this book apply as they do for people seeking an opposite sex partner.

I am referring to the problems that arise when someone is seeking an opposite sex marriage though they have same-sex preferences to a significant degree. This is not a problem where the person is comfortable enough with his or her sexuality to be direct with you about their needs and preferences. There are bisexual men and women who would be available to you for a meaningful long-term mating. If you can handle their sexual needs and what is often their inability to be monogamous (because there are periods when they prefer same-sex partners), they would be ranked as available. If not, rank them as unavailable.

Potential candidates are not, however, always that comfortable with themselves, or that direct with you. The problem is, how do you tell?

How Do You Tell?

When you are screening potential candidates for situational availability, the question really is, how do you know what their situation is? How do you know if they are married, separated, living with someone, not to mention the more delicate questions of sexual orientation or overinvolvements with mama?

There are three ways. The first is: If they don't volunteer the information, *ask for it.* Maybe it's a bit touchy to ask if someone is gay, but it is perfectly reasonable to inquire as to someone's living situation and legal status. Remember, it is in your interest and therefore up for you to assess availability to the extent that you can.

Yes, some people lie and asking will not prevent that. But a lie is easier by omission than commission. A certain percentage of people who will not feel responsible for informing you about their ongoing involvement, will balk at lying to you about it deliberately. Direct inquiry will protect you from the rationalizations and dodges of this group.

The second way to tell is one I've already mentioned: Focus on time. People otherwise involved are not likely to have as much time available for you. Time is objective and measurable. Don't ignore it.

Of course, neither of these strategies really helps to determine the degree of someone's attachment to a former mate, a family member, or a career. Nor is it an easy technique to use in evaluating someone's sexuality. In all of these areas you need the third technique, which is a particularly structured form of asking. I call it "Taking A Case History." Chapter 6 is about how to take such a history, what information to look for, and how to make sense of what you get.

Singles: The Available Group

The last group are those people available for a long-term relationship. They are legally single, currently uninvolved. Even within this group, some people are more available than others. This raises the question of psychological availability.

Once again the question of availability, this time psychological availability, is a more-or-less affair. It is much more difficult to evaluate than the situational availability. I raise it to make you aware that while the vast majority of adults marry in their lifetime (which is really a hopeful sign for you), at any given point in that lifetime someone is more or less available for making that move.

How do you evaluate someone's psychological availability? It's difficult, but some factors in the way people have set up their lives can give you a clue.

• What is the individual's history of long-term relationships?

Someone with a history of being willing to engage with one partner for some significant period of time is probably more available to do that with you than someone whose history runs in three-month cycles. The case history chapter will tell you how to get into this.

• Again, how much time is he or she willing to free up to invest in an intimate relationship?

• What do they say about themselves?

Most people have a system of rules for acting with integrity vis-à-vis another person. Unfortunately, some people's rule goes like this: I can act in any way I choose, as long as I've told you the score. This is not a problem when the way someone acts is consistent with what he or she says. If she tells you she's not looking for a committed relationship and she really limits the time she has for you . . . well, at least you know where you stand.

Unfortunately, many people use their words as an escape clause that permits them all sorts of intimate behavior. They say they're not interested in long-term involvement, yet they act like a potential mate, they invest all their time and emotional life in you. It's easy to ignore their words and concentrate on their behavior.

Don't do it. You must use both what people say *and* how they act as indications of psychological availability. You will notice that what someone says becomes more significant as the relationship progresses. Many people verbalize a disinclination toward marriage at the start of a relationship. There is a good deal of social pressure to do so. As we've discussed, you may be subject to and acting on this social pressure yourself. No one wants to scare someone away, so you might not have to take this initial verbal stance too seriously.

If it persists, however, don't ignore it. You have a goal in mind and if the other person repeatedly repudiates that goal, you've got a problem.

Consider Yourself

A note on psychological availability: What about your own? Remember, someone else has to pick you. You have to be out there and available for them to do it.

Are you?

Or are you home in front of the TV waiting for a magical phone call, or hung up on your married boss for whom you'd willingly stay late rather than have a dumb date with a stranger who got your number from your cousin. Perhaps you're hiding behind forty pounds of fat or a cynical posture and daring a loving person to come find you underneath.

It is not necessarily true that the fact that you haven't

found a mate means that you secretly don't want one. It may be true, however, that you have mixed feelings about finding a mate based on old scars, half understood fears, or familiar angers and disappointments. Sometimes people handle these mixed feelings by sabotaging themselves, by saying they want something but creating obstacles to getting it.

I suggest that you ask yourself this question: How available am I really? Follow it up with the corollary: If I feel I am available, do I act as if I am?

If you answered the earlier question—do I want to pick a mate?—with a yes (recognizing all your reservations: yes, but it has to be the right one; yes, but I won't die if I don't [you won't]; yes, but . . .) then review your behavior. Are you acting available?

Acting available is not the same as acting desperate, though they are easy to confuse. Being psychologically available yourself and following through on this psychological state with your behavior means this:

• You are willing to meet new people, to take part in the world outside your home or office.
• You have ended the go-nowhere relationship.

You have let go of the dead-end passion that has taken up so much of your psychological energy. I mean *ended* as in, you don't spend time with that person any more. I don't mean "thought about ending" as in "I'll stay with this person until someone better comes along." For someone else to come along and have you notice them, it helps to have something of a relationship vacuum in your life.

• You have stopped hiding behind your body.

You are hiding behind your body and making yourself unavailable if you are really fat, really sloppy, or really homely. No, you don't have to be thin, chic, or handsome to find a mate. (In fact, whether they're physically exquisite or physically flawed, people at both ends of the spectrum have trouble finding the right person.) You are simply aiming to get yourself away from the extremes of unacceptable into the wide normal range of people from where others pick mates.

• You have stopped carrying around a lot of anger.

Many people go through episodes, some of them lifelong, of being angry with the very group of people from whom they'd like to pick a mate. It is easy and in a certain way very natural to generalize your anger from one woman who shafted you to experiencing all women as manipulative. Or, conversely, to make the leap from one man who betrayed you to seeing all men as untrustworthy. You are not really available to a new mate until you are finished with your anger.

To repeat: The first rule in picking a mate is to begin a relationship with someone who is relatively available to be your mate.

The second general principle refers to an overall evaluation of a relationship with an eye toward its likelihood of developing into a lifelong one. It is a principle about the nature of relationships and what you will have to rethink and adjust to in the course of developing one. It goes like this:

Life is a blueplate special.
You want the chicken, it comes with the peas.
You want the roast beef, you get brussels sprouts.
NO SUBSTITUTIONS!

Rule #2: No Substitutions

Everyone is a package deal. If you want a mate, you buy the package. If you want a fantasy, you dream up a prince. It's a problem.

It's not an insoluble one, however. The trick is to have

such a clear assessment of the package you are buying that you can feel confident you got the better deal on balance. The "better deal" is an individual matter depending on what you have determined are your own requirements in a mate. Much of the rest of this book is devoted to helping you determine and perhaps rethink some of these requirements.

The point of Rule #2 is this: Whatever your priorities or your picture of a mate, what is true is that any candidate will inevitably bring with him or her some real obstacle (some unpleasant feature, something obnoxious) with which you will have to cope.

It is true that some of these characteristics can be changed through your benign influence. You *can* get him out of those awful plaid sports jackets and you *can* wean her from her boring addiction to French folk music. In fact, Chapter 6 discusses the question of what you can expect to change, how you might change it, and what you can expect to be stuck with forever.

None of the possibilities for change substantially alters Rule #2—No Substitutions. If you require that someone fulfill your perfect picture, and you are quickest to spot those areas where that person falls short, maybe the person you need to change is you. Otherwise, you're in for a long-term relationship with your fantasies.

You can comfort yourself against the harsh realities of Rule #2 with a single awareness. You too are a blue plate special. Someone will have plenty of adjusting to do when they mate with you. When you look at it that way, what could feel like compromise becomes nature's magical balance system.

Once you accept Rule #2, you will be orienting yourself toward a realistic appraisal of a potential mate. The first response to Rule #2 is usually a universal nod of agreement. Who could disagree, after all, with the idea that people are a complex package of strengths and weaknesses? After the nod of agreement comes a stream of protest.

There are usually three objections to turning such a rational eye on mating.

The first protest is a kind of primitive wail from the psyche. It takes the form of a loud internal "Yes, but . . ." I notice this objection most clearly in the discussions of Rule #2 in the classes and workshops I teach. The protest is what emerges when your intellectual appreciation of Rule #2 bangs smack up against your internal picture of who might be your mate.

By "picture" I mean your wish list. Your wish list is your perfectly clear or very tentative mental image of the kind of person with whom you'd like to form a lifelong relationship. Chapter 5 will help you to refine that picture and also help you to understand in what ways, for better or for worse, that picture has influenced your behavior. For now you need consider only one thing: That picture is invariably 100 percent positive. No one carries around an internally balanced picture, saying, "He'll be handsome and funny and he'll have trouble keeping a job" or "She'll be blonde, thin, and loud." Uh-Uh. Everyone's internal picture is rosy.

The obstacle that this mental picture presents to Rule #2 is a formidable one. When you begin an argument with the statement "Yes, but don't I have the right to expect . . ." or "Wouldn't she at least . . ." you are struggling with Rule #2.

If you can accept the reality of the rule, any changes your potential mate might make are icing on the cake. When you fight the rule, you tend to focus all your energy on the disappointing aspects of the relationship. If you want to struggle with them, you'll find plenty to struggle with in your search for perfection. On the other hand, if you can believe that reality is more fun and more satisfying than the fantasized ideal, and that, in fact, compromise and negotiation are more stimulating than utter agreement, the blow to your fantasies caused by Rule #2 won't be fatal.

The second protest against Rule #2 is one of attitude. Many people are reluctant to acknowledge what is negative, particularly at the beginning of a connection with somebody. The general idea is that if you force your attention toward the negative, you can inflate it. The corollary assumption would be that if you deny it, it will go away.

It just isn't so. If you are able to acknowledge the negative features that someone might bring to a marriage, you are closer to being able to accept them. Certainly you are closer to making a realistic assessment of whether you could live with these characteristics or not. The fact that there is a minus side must be acknowledged—but the role the minus side plays in an ongoing relationship is relative. If you let yourself know it, you can test out strategies for working around it. If you ignore the data, you have a time bomb planted in your marriage.

The third protest is rooted in all of your training and all of your brainwashing about the power of love itself. That's love as in "Love conquers all." If you rewrite that to reflect most people's experience, you'll get something like: "Love conquers all—for a while." In Chapter 6 we'll discuss "a while"—which I believe is approximately ninety days.

Does love erase all shortcomings and make all things possible? If it's the real thing, shouldn't it? The answer to both these question is: *No.* Love may be the grease that makes the friction over money or the laundry tolerable, but it will not make these conflicts disappear.

The way to minimize the importance of these conflicts is to assess their likelihood in advance and soften your attitude. This means really clarifying your priorities in a relationship, being clear about what you can and cannot live without.

Chapter 3 and 4 review the basic assumptions people make about marriage and suggest a model for evaluating a mate. Chapter 5 is designed to help you use this model to determine your own individual priorities. Read them to help you figure out what to do with the negative information once you've allowed yourself to know it.

One final note on the No Substitutions Rule. If you are over thirty, or seeking a mate who is over thirty, you are in for a startling discovery. Practically everyone is obviously flawed. This can be a special shock to the newly divorced person who was last in the market in his or her late teens or early twenties.

When you begin the cycle of mating at eighteen or twenty-two, nearly all the candidates are in good shape. First of all, they (and you) are in their physical prime. There are hardly any double chins or receding hairlines in the group. Compare this with the bodies over twenty-five that have begun their inevitable decline.

I am not referring to physical appearance alone: Lots of people in their thirties and forties and way beyond are great looking and much improved from the adolescent version of themselves.

But the older you are, the more likely you are to develop physical limitations. The back gets bad or the knee goes out and the stamina is generally not what it once was.

Not only do candidates come with more physical limitations, they come with more history. At twenty-two you are selecting a mate who is all potential; at thirty-five you are selecting an actual person. That person will inevitably appear at your doorstep with more psychological baggage than a person with a shorter past. He or she has experienced more failure, has a complicated set of long-term relationships into which you must fit, and probably has a history of more problems, simply because he or she has more history.

I point this out because newly divorced or separated people often respond to the single world with disappointment. "They're all turkeys." They're not. What they are is *older*, and life leaves its mark.

The thing to keep in mind is that most people over thirty

have something worrisome. Maybe they've fought alcoholism or survived the loss of a child or a marriage. Maybe they have a drug problem, or they're broke, or they have to support a senile parent. Whatever it is, they are likely to be a lot further from your ideal picture than the twenty-four-year-old you married the first time around.

What this suggests is that if you carry the same mental picture you had at eighteen of a potential mate, and the only alteration in it is a correction for the traits in your first mate that you learned to loathe, you will have a special problem with the idea of No Substitutions.

Once again you must take people as you find them. The older you find them, the more they bring with them, positive and negative. *No Substitutions.*

The question of love—that's love as in "Am I in love?" or "I still love her but I'm not in love" or "I want desperately to be in love"— is the central source of confusion in the selection of a mate.

"In love" is, by definition and strong preference, an irrational state. It is also temporary, though it can cycle through a long relationship. It is odd that people seek out a period of temporary insanity as the ideal mind-set for making a crucial life decision. It would be sensible to say "I can't decide whether to marry you or not. I'm too much in love to think clearly." Instead, people often feel that if they are not in the grip of this madness, something vital is lacking.

I do not mean to suggest that your emotional response is not a crucial factor in your selection of a mate. Rule #3 is the guiding principle for how to evaluate this emotional response.

Rule #3: How Do You Feel About You?

When evaluating your emotional response to a potential mate, focus your attention *not* on how you feel about him or her or how he/she feels about you, but on *how that person makes you feel about yourself.*

One of the things you marry is a version of yourself. Your mate is a mirror in which you see yourself reflected day after day. The picture you see does not have to be entirely compatible with the picture you carry around in your own mind. In other words, your mate does not have to see you exactly as you see yourself. What is important is that you have good feelings about yourself in reaction to how your potential mate sees you.

You see, love changes, particularly in the context of a real-life, ongoing situation. It does seem possible to maintain that do-or-die, Romeo-and-Juliet passion as long as passion is the only thing you share. But when budgets and chores and the kids' rebellion intervenes, love changes. To my way of thinking, this is no great loss on the reality level, although it can be a wrenching blow to one's fantasy life. I strongly recommend a shared life in the real world over a grand passion that requires separation, loneliness, and drama to sustain it. (No, you don't get both. Remember, *No Substitutions.*)

So love, in love, passionate love changes. It does not go away necessarily, but it does transmogrify to the point where it's sometimes hard to recognize. Therefore, it is quite difficult to use the information regarding how much love you feel for someone today, or how much you think is felt for you, as a rational predictor for how satisfactory your emotional life will be with that someone as your mate.

Rule #3 is a much more reliable criterion. The question of how you feel about yourself is often overlooked. First of all there is some resistance, even in psychological literature, to the idea that another person can influence your feelings for yourself. There is the wishful notion that each of us could have such a strong, intact, fully-developed self-image that it would be impervious to the distortions of another person's views.

Unfortunately, it's not true. Aren't there people who see

you as smart or funny, around whom you relax into being as smart and funny as you can be? Whereas for someone else you are nobody special and you come away from that person feeling exactly that: Nobody special.

In the matter of picking your relationships in the world, how you are seen is a critical factor in how you will behave. In the matter of picking a mate, this has more significance still.

To a large extent you will live with and take on your mate's attitude toward you. If he sees you as helpless and flaky (which he doesn't mind, he likes to feel strong and needed), you may experience yourself as incompetent. How does that feel to you? If she sees you as stolid and mature (she likes to think of you as someone with no surprises), how do you respond to that?

No one else can decide which picture of you should make you feel positive about yourself. The important issue is that, whatever creates it, you should feel very good about yourself in the context of your relationship with your mate. Of course, you can't feel this way 100 percent of the time. Sometimes you blow it, your mate confronts you and you feel rotten, small, and guilty.

I am speaking of your sense of yourself overall. Does your prospective mate's view of you increase your self-respect? Does his or her attraction to you help you feel attractive? Does that person bring out or enhance the things you consider your strengths? Does he or she soften your failures and shore up your weaknesses? Are you a better version of yourself as *you* experience it because of your connection? This is tricky. I'm not advocating a parental type of mating, where you act better because someone is around to make you toe the line. In that situation, you might behave like a better version of yourself but feel like a bad kid. I am referring to how much you like the self you are with this person and how good you feel about the self you see.

The emotional relationship you have with yourself is the

central pivot around which an intimate relationship with someone else turns. You are freer to love, forgive, compromise, or change for someone else when the sense you get about yourself for doing it is terrific. Furthermore, you can tolerate a good deal of disappointment and hard times when you love the experience of yourself as seen by the person who is closest to you.

It's obvious that some people connect with others primarily to confirm a negative sense they have about themselves. The result of these pairings is often psychological or physical abuse. To oversimplify, because this is not a book on abused mates, there are people who cannot tolerate a person who sees them in a positive light. They seek out partners who will confirm their negative images of themselves. This approach to mating is part of a formula for a very unhappy life. If you recognize yourself in this, please seek out professional counseling.

The vast majority of us carry around a mixed, and to some degree, uncertain sense of who we are. A mate can go a long way toward influencing that in one direction or another. Pick the person who pushes your sense of yourself in a positive direction.

How to Use These Rules

It's clear that these three rules on availability, substitutions, and emotion relate to three different steps in the mating process. They are meant as guidelines, directing your attention to the different phases of a relationship.

Rule #1, availability, is meant to be a screening technique. At the very least, Rule #1 should be used to help you clarify your purpose. Are you looking for a fling, a relationship, or a mate? All relationships are not of the mating variety. If you'd like a mate, you will save yourself a good deal of effort and anguish if you use Rule #1 scrupulously.

The stuff of life is time and time in life is finite. You have a limited amount of psychological energy to invest in other people and the development of a relationship uses up both your store of that energy and the time you have available. Invest it wisely.

Rule #1 is intended to be a rational approach to that investment. The advantage of focusing on availability is that you can benefit from your ability to reason before you are in the grips of a dead-end situation. You can get one-up on your customary emotional pitfalls. Try it.

Rule #2, no substitutions, reflects a fundamental truth about the nature of relationships. It is meant to help you include a whole picture at a time when your feelings and fantasies will conspire to make you ignore certain realities.

These realities never stay submerged forever. In fact, they tend to emerge later as major disappointments or significant obstacles to working on a real marriage once a mate has been selected. The purpose of Rule #2 is twofold: First, to help you accept the reality that where people are concerned, there is no perfection. There is no princess or prince waiting for you at the next turn in the road, next bar, or next blind date. There are only other people, some better suited to you than others. The second purpose is to help you gather appropriate information early in the relationship so that you can evaluate the nature of the compromise you will be required to make. And you will be required to make one. All marriages are a series of negotiations and compromises. It's just so much easier to make them gracefully when you know about them in advance and have decided you can live with them.

Rule #3, on emotion, offers a particular guide to the evaluation of your feeling state because, after all, feelings are the basis of an intimate relationship.

Rule #3 directs your attention to an area of feeling in a relationship that is most often ignored: your feeling for yourself. This rule reminds you that while your feelings for someone else are difficult to measure, your feelings about yourself are a steadier barometer. Once you focus your thoughts in this direction, you will likely find a lot of overlooked information about the nature of your relationship and the likelihood of its being a satisfactory one for you on a lifetime basis.

The three golden rules should form the nucleus of your operating principles as you choose a mate. You don't have to take them on faith. But I urge you to try them out and see how they work for you. They've helped a lot of other people go through the mating process more smoothly. They could help you.

·3·

Rich and Sexy

Ordinarily, I'd be the last person to tell you not to listen to your mother. But when it comes to picking a mate, you'd do better to keep in mind the advice of Hans Christian Andersen. Your mother will be able to tell you who qualifies as a good catch. Hans Christian Andersen reminds you to *beware of the emperor's new clothes*.

You probably remember the story. The emperor appeared before the town in a magic outfit, visible only to those important enough to see it. Naturally, everyone vastly admired his apparel. The only exception was a child who, too innocent to recognize the importance of being important, stated the truth—the emperor was naked.

The social "catch" is too often like the emperor—naked, but no one will admit it. The best thing you can do for yourself is to be that child.

When the whole world is pretty much in agreement about what makes a desirable mate, it's tough for you to rethink the whole question for yourself. Part of what makes it so tough is that you are bucking an astonishing amount of social consensus. But you must. Otherwise you spend all your time looking for the emperor.

The earliest representatives of our species (that's going back some forty thousand years) had fairly permanent matings. Forty thousand years of experience is plenty of time to form some pretty strong opinions about how to pick a mate.

As a member of that society, you are inundated by those opinions from birth. You may experience them as your father's opinions or the views of your best friend Patrick, as Nora Ephron's opinions, or cousin Jane's. In reality these are the opinions of society-at-large, handing down its cultural values from one generation to another. It is what we mean by folklore or folk wisdom. As a first step toward understanding what you are looking for when you choose a mate, it helps to understand what society tells you to look for, and *why* it makes these assumptions.

The Biological Imperative

The answers all lie in biology.

For thousands of years, three biological facts shaped our social world:

1. For human groups to survive amongst animals that were stronger and faster, they had to use their one biological advantage—their brains. Those brains had the ability to *organize the group* under the strongest, smartest, and most talented. Establishing dominance in the social group was a matter of biological survival.

2. Human females, unlike their animal ancestors, don't have a rutting season. They are sexually available pretty much all of the time.

3. Human babies need long-term care. Someone has to stay home with them to ensure their survival.

These three biological facts determined the human social structure. While shaping that structure, humans were also taught some strong assumptions about desirable mates.

As Ralph Linton points out in "The Natural History of the Family," if you put these three facts together, here's what happens: you have a group of males, fighting out a dominance hierarchy, who are confronted with females, now, like the males, available to have sex most of the time. One strategy for males to establish dominance is to claim a desirable female.

Add to the desire to claim a female the requirements of the offspring. Any species that has developed dependent infants had better develop a stable social group to take care of them, or that species won't last more than a generation.

Human society had to organize into some structure that could take care of the babies, provide for the individual who was furnishing the care, and defend the whole group in the process. Human society did just that, and the structure is called the family.

Think about it. Let's say you're a female fish. Your babies zip out of their eggs and swim away to get their own food. How convenient for you. You are free to get food for yourself and you don't need a stable mate to look after you while you look after the babies.

If, on the other hand, you are a career couple living, let's say, twenty thousand years ago, you were pretty much stuck. The kid can't feed itself, it can't hunt, why, it can't even lift its little head for a while. Its survival, then, is your responsibility.

This is no light observation when you consider that a human female in the natural state (i.e. before birth control via chemical, mechanical, or social means) bore a child on the average of once every eighteen months! Of course, her life expectancy wasn't much to write home about, but then neither was anyone else's.

The female of childbearing years was thus, of biological and social necessity, removed from the work world outside the home. The work world for pre-agricultural man was largely the hunting and gathering of materials necessary for survival: food, skins for clothing, shelter. The human female was dependent on her mate to gather these things for her.

The male was equally dependent. He couldn't very well hunt or gather while he was taking care of babies. Beyond that, he needed someone to turn the raw materials into things he could use. It's one thing to slay a bison, quite another thing to cook it.

If you were a cave lady, it was easy to see that the highly desirable mates were the ones who were most skilled at bringing home the raw materials. They were the best hunters, the strongest, wiliest gatherers, the ones from strong, well-organized families who were willing to share the wealth. They were likely to be the dominant members of the tribe or clan, the ones who held the most status. And, in turn, they conveyed the most status on their mates. You know who they were—they were the rich ones.

That's rich as in "It's just as easy to fall in love with a rich man as a poor one," or "He's not so short when he stands on his money."

The dominant cavemen, who occupied high status in the group, were also looking to mate. They too needed to be part of this basic economic unit in order to survive and to ensure the survival of their offspring. As an expression of their dominance, and a further reinforcement of their status, these males chose the most desirable females. The definition of desirable becomes obvious. Those who were most sexually attractive, whose mating would deprive the other males in the tribe of their favors, were clearly the first choice. Add to that the needs for a tranquil, organized home and good cooking and you have the origins of the following kinds of folk wisdom: "The way to a man's heart is through his stomach," and "A lady in the living room and a whore in the bedroom," and "Cooking lasts, kissing don't."

You have the original perfect "10." She was the sexiest

one and everyone wanted her. She cooked, she sewed, she cleaned, she took great care of the kids, and she was always ready to make love.

There you have, if in rather capsulized cartoon form, the origins of the classic assumptions society makes about desirable mates: Rich and Sexy.

These are both meant as broadly inclusive terms. "Rich" does not refer simply to money. Rich can mean in actual material resources, in social status, power, or all three. It refers to those males who, by virtue of their material worth, their skill and daring, and/or their family connections, occupy a position of some significance in the world.

"Sexy" is a term that also covers a lot of ground. Sexy here means highly sexually desirable (by whatever standards, fashion being what it is) as well as highly competent at all of women's traditional economic contributions: Child care, creation and maintenance of the home, cooking, making the clothes. The woman with a highly desirable anatomy and the skill and temperament to do her job well was a very sexy woman.

The biological imperatives of Rich and Sexy still form the basis of our assumptions about desirable mates today. If anything has changed at all, it is the gender distinctions in these requirements. Women have learned to demand sexy males, men have learned to seek out rich women. For both men and women, Rich and Sexy is still the clarion cry of the single adult.

The biological, social, and economic pressures that highly value Rich and Sexy were not the only criteria for mating, even in primitive times. The psychological needs we'll discuss in the next section were also operating principles for primitive man, though to a lesser extent. But it is fair to argue that for primitive man, these were the main considerations for choosing a mate.

What is astonishing is the extent to which these standards endure as assumptions about desirable mates today.

You will need to check these out with yourself. Try not to be too defensive about it, as if I've accused you of being shallow. I know that you have lots of requirements for a mate besides Rich and Sexy. I am simply asking you to wonder aloud to what degree these play a role in your own criteria, and particularly in your screening techniques.

Women and men might both plead that they are not seeking a rich mate. I suggest you be less literal about the word *rich*. It is really referring to social status and to the perception of power.

I've met few men and fewer women for whom social status is not an automatic screening principle. Whatever your standard, you determine rapidly if someone meets it, making a swift assessment of dress, speech, style, and occupation. ("What do you do?" is *not* just casual social chit-chat.) If someone passes this preliminary screening, you may pursue the relationship. If they fail, they are "beneath me," "not our kind, darling," or "not my type." In fact, you may not even *notice* someone as a potential candidate who doesn't give off the right social class signals.

Sexy works the same way. You follow whatever standard you've developed. Most commonly, it's a standard you've set in conjunction with the rest of your social group. The idea of having a partner who is seen as sexually desirable by your group, but who is exclusively yours, is still a pretty powerful one. You rule out those potential partners who don't measure up.

What's wrong with that? If this person's going to be my sexual partner, you say, I've got to find him sexy. If we are going to be an economic unit, I sure want to know she's going to hold up her end. If I am going to be completely economically dependent, I want to make sure he or she can provide me with a comfortable life.

There's nothing wrong with it. But there is a liability connected with these assumptions to which you should be alerted.

The cut-off point for rich enough and sexy enough is set more by your group than by you individually.

It happens over and over again. Perhaps it's happened to you. You fall in love with the "wrong" person.

This can be an agonizing situation. The "wrong" person can of course be the wrong one because he or she treats you badly, makes you miserable, or drives you crazy. That's not the kind of "wrong" I mean here.

I mean socially wrong, someone who looks wrong, someone with whom you feel funny at parties because your friends are so carefully non-judgmental. This wrong person is, you feel, too fat, too funny-looking, too low-class, too other-class, the wrong religion, ethnicity, age. You are soul mates privately, but you can't really see him or her as part of your world.

Obviously, this person is okay by you for many things or you wouldn't be enjoying the relationship as much as you are. But you simply will not receive the social status in the group that you want a mate to deliver.

What to do? You love him, but he's kind of a bum. You love her, but your friends think she's a dog. These are tough social hurdles to overcome.

Many people sidestep these conflicts by avoiding socially unacceptable partners. Most of us try to avoid them by using socially acceptable screening standards and sticking with them. You don't want to risk warming to the wrong kind of person and perforce choosing between personal satisfaction and social status.

Yes, this is the argument taken to its extreme. Yes, you do have certain sexual tastes and preferences and it is important that these be satisfied. Yes, you will be economically interdependent with your mate, and it's important to know that he or she can make enough to survive comfortably. Just consider how much of what you require to suit you sexually or economically is what *you* truly require, and how much is what you think you are socially expected to have.

Remember, please yourself.

The Psychological Quest

The biologically based criteria of Rich and Sexy are in no way the only items on the list of desirable traits in a mate. In a way you'd be better off if they were, because you wouldn't have the problem of working out this dreadfully difficult thing called a Relationship-with-a-capital-R.

They never were the only requirements on the list. Humans are social animals and their psychological needs have always coexisted with their biological necessities. Those psychological needs are real and powerful.

We know that humans require more than the maintenance of their basic biological needs to survive. Babies in orphanages who are fed and cleaned, but who don't receive a lot of touching and attention, sometimes exhibit what's called failure to thrive. In fact, they may die for no apparent organic reason. We know that psychological needs for warmth, love, and human contact are crucial for actual survival.

The psychological needs for survival are various and complicated. For the sake of giving you an overview, I will summarize them, as Linton does, into three categories.

They are, essentially:

- a need for security in personal relationships
- a need for congenial companionship
- a need for intimacy

Security is the sense that you are safe with someone, that that person values you highly and cares for your well-being. It is the sense that you trust his or her basic regard for you, for your feelings, for your self-esteem. It is knowing that that person will be available to you on a continuous basis.

The need for security is the source of a lot of the anxiety about infidelity. Infidelity is a threat less because of the sexual act itself, than the threat it represents to the security of a continuously available relationship. Sexual infidelity means, for a lot of people, that their partner went away briefly and could potentially go away permanently. Whether the partner really intends to leave or not is irrelevant. The threat to security can be devastating. It is not devastating because you are necessarily personally insecure or have poor self-esteem. It is ruinous because you are human and human beings require security in their closest relationships for psychological survival.

This does not mean it is impossible to be secure without monogamy. Some people are able to readjust their thinking so that sexual relationships do not represent a threat to the commitment between themselves and their partners. They strive to make this adjustment in their thinking in order to allow themselves and their partners fuller or more diversified sexual experiences. It's a legitimate goal if active, varied sexual experiences are a high priority for you both. But in our culture, it's a really tough mental leap to make. To do it well usually requires two like-minded people who have reason to believe that their union is locked in cement and that sexual activity is mainly for fun and not a primary expression of the union.

Nice work if you can get it. Otherwise, stay away. Emotional security is a psychological necessity of happy mating.

So is congenial companionship. The human being has a need to be with others, to share leisure, opinions, work, and attitudes with other human beings in a pleasant way. We want to like other people and have them like us. We want to share our interests with people. We need playmates.

It's important to us that our mate be able to provide some of this. Actually, people often expect their mates to fulfill most or all of this need. That's a problem that requires constant balancing between the need to have congenial companions and the need for security. Your need to feel secure can make your mate's choice of congenial companionship other than yourself a real source of anxiety. However the two of you resolve the balancing act, you will need to have a high degree of companionship in your relationship, and in your life, to feel psychologically satisfied.

Finally, humans need *intimacy.* This means we have a psychological need for someone to be in tune with us emotionally. Our mate needs to know how we feel about things, what triggers these feelings and most of all, what we need from someone else when we are feeling a particular way.

This psychological craving for intimacy is probably not as ancient an expectation as the needs for emotional security and companionship. It is more a result of the changes in the way we live and the way we were raised as children.

Increasingly, our society has narrowed its emotionally intimate networks. Where once we lived amid large social groups or with generations of families under one roof, we have moved in the direction of smaller and smaller units.

When you are raised in a single intense relationship with a parent, as most children in our society are, you learn early that one person should be available to meet your emotional needs for warmth, contact, attention, for love itself.

With this kind of childhood experience, it is perfectly natural for you to transfer these expectations to your search for a mate. When you come to that point in life where you are separating your emotional attachments from your parents and looking to form a new family, what you'll expect that new person to offer is very much like what you were offered as a child.

Unfortunately, I mean that quite literally—which is why psychotherapists are called upon so often. I also mean it in a more general sense. You anticipate that you will have one significant relationship that will be a large part of the source of your warmth, love, and affection in the world. You've been conditioned to expect that one person will get to be very close to you, will get to understand you, will know your moods, know your feelings, know what you need. You expect this whether or not your mother gave it to you or however successfully she fulfilled it. There is still the sense that one person is the primary object, the primary figure who is the source of your emotional gratification on these crucial issues. When you look for a mate you need to find a lot of the same things.

We all live now in such a painfully transistory world. We don't stay in the same neighborhood, or same job, for a lifetime. Our great-great grandparents did. They had the opportunity to know any number of people intimately, over the course of a lifetime. They could count on being connected to several generations on a daily basis. Their economic and physical worlds afforded them many more opportunities for psychologically satisfying, secure, and intimate relationships with others.

It's not so anymore. In our mobile, twentieth-century America, the story of our relationships is largely a story of loss. We leave the families that knew us and go to live among strangers. We reduce family relationships to twice-a-year visits. When the urge comes to reach out and touch someone, what we touch is a telephone.

We learn to expect the loss of beloved friends in the same way. They move away, or we do, following the ebb and flow of new jobs, new housing, new and more central relationships. Eventually we lose our children, as we lost the tight bond to our own parents. I don't mean we lose the love or the concern. But we lose the daily gratification, the satisfaction of sharing our thoughts and feelings with those who have a shot at really knowing us, our history. We are constantly starting over.

There is only one relationship in our adult lives that offers us the real possibility of being known over a long-term period. That is our mate. This is the person who moves when we do, who is sharing the new house, the new environment. The mate becomes our likeliest possibility for gratifying the need we developed out of our childhood, the need for intimacy.

Changing Realities: From the Biological
Imperative to the Psychological Quest

There's been a big shift over time in the importance of the biological needs and psychological needs.

For early humans, the biological needs were dominant and all of the family structures that resulted from them were really a matter of biological survival.

I've already discussed how the original idea behind "family" is less crucial for the fulfillment of biological needs. Our society has been restructured so that you don't have to have a woman in your home to get food on the table and you don't have to have a man out in the world earning your money. There are other ways to survive biologically than within the traditional family unit.

Interestingly, the part that has not changed has been the dependence of children. In fact, it has lengthened. Anthropologists used to agree that dependence ended with the acquisition of pubic hair. Today, it lingers until the acquisition of an M.B.A. But the solutions to this problem have increased enormously.

The survival problem still confronts us. But the available solutions are radically different.

At the very least there are:

- more individual options around whether we have children, and how many
- more control over when in our life span we decide to have children
- more choices about child care for those dependent children

- more ways to provide food, clothing, and habitable shelter than the simple dependence on a female
- more economic opportunities for women to earn their own raw materials for survival.

At the same time that these biologically-based motivations for mating have declined, the psychological motivations for mating have increased.

The underlying longings for the fulfillment of our emotional needs were less driving for our ancestors partly because they were easier to gratify. People lived in groups and human contact was simply an easier thing. It's just not as easy when you're living in your junior one-bedroom.

We live in an increasingly isolated, mechanized world. We live apart from others. We often live alone. You could go from Friday night to Monday morning without hearing a human voice that didn't come through your television set, unless you go to the grocery store. Sometimes you do go to the grocery store just to have another living person ask you how you are.

The urge for human contact can become as compulsive as the drive for sex itself. Have you ever been sitting at home and you're just driven to the telephone and you're really trying to think of someone to call? That's an expression of the need for affiliation. Some people go through periods where they're in such an isolated funk that they almost lose the ability to make that kind of contact. They get locked within themselves. It's not for nothing that you're saying there's no place to meet anyone anymore. It *is* harder to make contact. It's harder to have people around who really know you. It's infinitely harder to develop with someone that feeling of intimacy so necessary for psychological survival.

As the biological imperatives have become less important, the psychological needs have become more driving.

Have You Made the Shift?

Old values and attitudes die a much slower death than the social institutions on which they are based. You may be a member of this twentieth-century society who still operates on the selection strategies of your primitive ancestors.

If your primary reason for mating is to ensure the biological survival of yourself and your offspring, Rich and Sexy belong at the top of your list of desirable traits in a mate. You have needs for psychological satisfaction as well, but these are clearly secondary.

But, if you live in a world where you can survive biologically and so can your kids, without a mate, Rich and Sexy are less important. If your need for a mate is a matter of your psychological survival, your priorities change. Rich and Sexy are still on the list, but they are no longer number one. They are replaced by someone's ability to satisfy your emotional needs.

Have you paid attention to this shift in needs when you set out to choose a mate? The easiest way to check this out is to observe the kind of responses you have when you meet someone.

What is most typical is that you screen out potential candidates based on the age-old biological imperative: Could this person provide for me? Do I find this person sexually attractive? After you've screened people out on these criteria, you then become concerned with something called The Relationship. Can we be close, can we trust each other, can I feel safe, do they offer me love, do I love them, do I feel warmth, affection, can we be companions?

Isn't that crazy? If the real function of a mate is psychological support, why would your first screening be for biological survival? The answer is very easy. That's what you learned, that's what you've been doing forever, and that's what you're still doing.

Besides that, this outdated screening strategy is the simplest. You have to open yourself up to a great many people, over a period of time, to know whether they can be psychologically fulfilling for you. It's a facile tool simply to decide whether someone is sexually your type or offers you enough social status to bother pursuing the relationship. Most people would be quite willing to say that "nobody's perfect," or "no one has everything on the list." They're happy taking a reasonable attitude that they want a mate who fulfills their primary requirements. The problem is that the primary requirements you've been trained to seek are not really the primary requirements that someone will ultimately have to fulfill to satisfy you.

The *problem* you're running up against is inevitable when you screen people first for their standing in the world and second for their relationship to you.

This lag in your thinking, this overemphasis on old values, is the biggest *difficulty* people have in choosing the correct mate.

The next chapter is a formula for learning to overcome this problem.

·4·

How to Pick a Mate

Try this exercise: Think of yourself as someone else's potential candidate for a mate. (You are, you know.)

Don't do this exercise in one of your exaggerated down-on-yourself moods. Wait until you're feeling relaxed and comfortable with yourself. Then answer these questions:

Why would someone want you as a mate?

1.	6.
2.	7.
3.	8.
4.	9.
5.	10.

Why wouldn't they?

1.	6.
2.	7.
3.	8.
4.	9.
5.	10.

I know you sometimes skip over exercises and read ahead to find out what it all means. That's okay most of the time. But for this exercise to be of any real use to you, stop and do it right now. We'll discuss your answers later in this chapter.

A Model for Choosing a Mate

This chapter is going to teach you how to turn your thinking upside down. It's the stuff your family may not have told you, the secret strategy for pleasing yourself.

All you have to do is make a simple shift in your attitude that will bring you in line with what is true about relationships in the late twentieth century. The truth is that a mate who fulfills your emotional needs is more important to you than one who can pay your bills, cook your meals, or be a knockout at your college reunion. We have developed from a world where you needed a partner just to survive from day to day to a world where you can handle survival on your own. Your partner's purpose is to help you maximize your happiness.

You will be able to make this shift most efficiently if you consider the social and psychological criteria for choosing a mate as two separate categories. I've organized them for you in a chart on p. 69.

Category #1 points out how the world at large evaluates a candidate. It includes all of those externally observable, measurable traits that are of value to your social group. These standards are derived from the biological necessities we discussed in Chapter 3. They are the traditional measures of Rich and Sexy: physical appearance, occupation, material possessions, manner of dress, and general life-style. You'll notice that for every social qualification in Category #1, there is a parallel psychological qualification in Category #2.

Category #2 measures someone's relationship to you. It focuses your attention on all of those psychological needs that are not immediately obvious. Indeed, they may never be apparent to the world at large. But they are the key to evaluating how satisfying a relationship might be *for you.*

Later in this chapter, I will demonstrate how to use this model to screen a room of strangers successfully. First, you must understand it in detail, and overcome some internal obstacles to using it.

Biologically-Derived Criteria: (Who They Are in the World)	Psychologically-Derived Criteria: (Who They Are with You)
Judged by:	Judged by:
Degree of Physical Attractiveness	Degree of Sexual Satisfaction
Educational Level	Intelligence
Income	Degree of Intimacy
Profession/Occupation	Shared Interests/ Companionship
General Life-Style— Home, Vacation, Social Network, Style of Dress, Props	General Personality Style—Warmth, Compatibility, Sense of Humor, Communication Skills, Maturity, Temperament
Family—Religion—Age:	The Givens

• Note the difference between physical attractiveness as it conforms to the values of the group, and degree of sexual satisfaction someone offers to you. You can be sexually compatible with all sorts of different people. Only a narrow range of those people will be highly valued by your group.

• Educational level may or may not be an indication of intelligence. Intelligence is where the fun is: education is what happened in the past. It's tempting to eliminate people who are, in your opinion, under- or over-educated. Why worry about it at all?

• Income is pretty straightforward—the more the better. Don't forget, the same holds true for intimacy.

• The candidate's profession indicates what he or she does when not with you. Shared interests indicate what you are likely to do together. Don't screen people out first because you don't admire their outside life. Screen them out first because you wouldn't enjoy your time with them.

• It's true that you will share a life-style (it's also true that you will help to make a new one), which makes the potential candidate's current life-style of particular interest. Don't forget that his or her personality will have more impact on you than life-style. The impact of personality is just harder to measure, which makes it easier to ignore.

• Family, ethnic group, race, religion, and age are all determinants for which your social group has relatively strict rules. You may have to consider breaking some of them to satisfy your other needs.

• "Respect" is not on either list, though many of you feel strongly that you must respect someone as well as love them. It's true, you must.

Respect is often a by-product of watching someone live up to your standards. You may have trouble respecting a woman who chooses not to have children, or a man with an insignificant job. Or, you might evaluate these candidates by a whole different standard and respect them for their independence. Respect is a result of knowing what you want and appreciating what you get.

Both categories in the chart count. Both are important. What you need is a strategy for using them.

I think what you've probably been doing to this point is setting fairly narrow standards on category #1, the social scale, then hoping to find someone psychologically satisfying who passes your social screening. You run into several problems, however, when you take this approach, problems that significantly reduce the likelihood of finding the right person for your mate.

When you go for the two-from-column-A, Chinese-menu-style of seeking a mate, you significantly increase the competition without significantly increasing your chances for happiness.

You increase your chances of competition because you go for the same social externals that everyone else is going for. Perhaps you and your friends differ on some minor points (blonde versus redhead, full-breasted versus lean, three-piece suit versus leather jacket), but you are all fairly locked into a standard that decides what is "physically attractive." The same is true about standards on occupational status, income, education, family background. We have a clear value system around these aspects of life. It's not hard to determine roughly who ranks above whom on each of these counts. You might have to choose which has priority for you—looks or income. (Traditionally, men are encouraged to go for looks, while women opt for income.) Ideally, you seek candidates who have some acceptable degree of each. When you are assured of their acceptability, you move on to explore the possibilities for psychological satisfaction.

People often protest their independence on these issues, saying "I don't care what my friends think, but he or she has to be attractive to *me.*" This assumes that your form your ideas about what is attractive independently—as if you are not part of a social group and strongly influenced by it.

Social criteria are just too powerful and too clear to ignore. They are the easiest to judge, and the easiest to be objective about. They are also the easiest to compete over. Besides decreasing your chances of finding someone in the first place, social screening criteria increase your chances of finding the wrong person.

It's a painfully disappointing phenomenon. You are trained to seek a mate according to who he or she is as an individual in the world at large rather than who he or she is to you. Unfortunately, these are often very different. And what makes "the world" happy may not make *you* happy at all.

Why Can't I Have Both?

Of course you want both the status and the satisfaction. Why shouldn't you? Who wouldn't?

You may feel you deserve both. Perhaps you feel that you yourself offer strengths from both sides of our Chinese menu. You are admittedly attractive, bright, and gainfully employed. Your family is respectable, your formal education complete. You also feel you are warm, loving, and capable of satisfying someone in bed, if it's the right someone. You are bright and caring, trustworthy. You deserve at least that in return.

Will you get it? Some people seem to, or least it seems so when you look at their relationship from the outside. It's very easy to misread other couples, particularly when you, as part of the social group, evaluate these mates through society's external standards.

Naturally, you'd like to have everything. But consider for a moment: Do *you* have everything to offer? Will you really be offering such a panoply of assets to the person who chooses you? Maybe, but it's doubtful. So much of the way we see ourselves distorts our own limitations. Most of us are more aware of someone else's shortcomings than we are of our own. We understand ourselves, make excuses for ourselves. We are protective of our own feelings. ("I can say something bad about me, but don't *you* say something bad about me. I'll defend myself. I don't like to have to admit that I'm wrong.")

That's why I put exercise #2 ("Why *wouldn't* someone want you as a mate. . .") at the beginning of this chapter. (We'll discuss exercise #1 later.) To develop a more realistic picture of what you need from a mate, it helps to have a clear view of what someone has to put up with in you.

I don't have a formula to discuss your ten answers; this is not a quiz. It's an exercise in self-awareness. I just suggest that you take a look at your list, try to finish it if you haven't. Yes, there really are ten less-than-wonderful things about you that your mate will have to accept. You can probably make a fair guess right now about which of these limitations you'll be able to change and which your mate will have to live with forever.

Exercise #2 is only apparently simple—you'll need to review your list carefully.

I've noticed that in this exercise, people mention shortcomings that are really compliments in disguise. For example: I asked my colleague, Eric, to complete this exercise. His answers reflect the perverse pride that a lot of men show when they're asked to be self-critical. Here are his answers to the question "Why wouldn't someone want you as a mate?"

1. I smoke too much
2. I drink too much
3. I work too much
4. I'm intolerant of mediocrity
5. I get bored easily
6. I *can't stand* bullshit
7. I abhor playing games
8. I'm into making it successfully—business-wise
9. I'm outspoken to the degree of harm
10. I'm condescending

Look at #4. His admission of a fault is really an announcement of his pursuit of excellence. Number #6 is an advertisement of his integrity and #7 of his directness. With faults like these, who needs virtues?

Men do seem to have more difficulty with self-criticism but they're not entirely alone. Take a look at Alexis' list.

1. My tastes are too expensive
2. I'm a perfectionist
3. I like to do things a certain way
4. I tell it like it is
5. I like to keep going
6. I have two kids

Alexis gave up on her list at this point. She paused, then wrote: "I think all these things are positive."

The reality is that few, if any of us, have a completely desirable package to offer. If you don't have it to offer, how come you still keep getting mad that you can't find it in someone else?

The answer to whether you can have both the status and satisfaction seems to be—yes and no. Yes, anyone who could be your mate will have to demonstrate qualities that are acceptable to some degree on both sets of needs. But no, no one will meet all of your highest expectations on both sides of the chart. You will be disappointed, or forced to compromise on some feature or other. I urge you to save your compromises for the social end.

Right now you are setting up fairly rigid standards concerning someone's standing in the group. Then, from the pool of people who pass this screening, you explore the facets of a personal relationship. Implicit in this approach is that you value someone's social standing in the world as the most important feature in a mate. You are stuck back in the old biological assumptions of Rich and Sexy.

To understand how you yourself wish to be judged go back and review exercise #1 at the beginning of this chapter. You listed ten qualities or facets of yourself and your life that described why you felt you were desirable as a mate.

Rewrite your list here:

1.   6.
2.   7.
3.   8.
4.   9.
5.   10.

Mark each item either S, for a trait that increases your desirability in the social group, or P, for a trait that offers something to an intimate relationship. Count up your number of S's and P's. Perhaps your lists will look something like these.

Marine, a 36-year-old divorced woman's list:

S or P (depending how she meant it)	1. smart
P	2. competent
S	3. pretty
S	4. good cook
P	5. good companion
P	6. thoughtful
P	7. loyal
P	8. hardworking
P	9. honest
"Oh yes, I forgot sex . . ."	
P	10. passionate

Here is Michael's list. He's 41, divorced, the captain and owner of a charter boat company he's just getting off the ground.

P	**1.** responsible
P	**2.** energetic
P	**3.** communicative
S	**4.** goal-oriented
P	**5.** sexual
P	**6.** romantic
P	**7.** family-oriented
P	**8.** problem solver
P	**9.** diplomatic
S	**10.** tasteful

You'll probably find, as these people did, that you have a lot more P's than S's. Clearly you would prefer to be judged by what you have to offer in a relationship than by your social standing. Making the screening shift away from an emphasis on someone's standing in your social group and toward how satisfying someone is in relationship to you, will be easier when you understand that you would prefer to be evaluated by these criteria yourself.

Even with this shift in priorities, you still need to screen potential candidates efficiently and reliably to conserve your time and energy. And yet, the only information available to you at first glance are those external, social, unreliable criteria.

How do you use your external criteria to maximize the possibility of a psychologically satisfying relationship? It's simple. Just widen your selection standards in column #1.

Turn 2 Out of 10 to 8 Out Of 10

Here's what's probably happening now: You go to a party (a bar, a circus, who cares). You're operating on a set of built-in standards and you use these to screen the room. These standards are, invariably, socially conscious standards, evaluating social position in the world at large. They are external criteria. They have to be. The psychological standards simply can't be assessed very reliably at first glance.

You scan the room. (You scan your life.) With the socially conscious criteria you've developed, possibly two out of ten potential candidates pass the screening. Based on some fixed ideas, prejudices, and social stereotypes, you've eliminated 80 percent of the pool.

Here's a better strategy. Out of every ten possible candidates, two will fall into your immediately-acceptable category. There will be two whose looks or style appeal to you, or possibly whose reputation has preceded them and intrigued you. (Let's face it, if Henry Kissinger showed up unrecognized at a cocktail party, you wouldn't exactly cream. If you knew it was Henry Kissinger, it might give you pause for thought.)

So the top two are easy. Of course, the fact that your top two might be everyone's top two *is* a bit of a problem. That's the competition I mentioned earlier.

It seems reasonable to me that out of a pool of ten, two people will simply be off the list as far as your social standards go. You're entitled to that. The potential candidates will be simply too sloppy, too old, too young, too fat, too poor, too hippy, too "low class," too loud. These two people get eliminated as unacceptable because of your interpretation of their standing in the world. At the end of this chapter we will work on fine-tuning your criteria for eliminating these two.

But what about the other six? Usually you ignore them because you've focused on your top two. If you are really willing to shift your attention from socially acceptable criteria to your internal psychological needs, you will also be shifting your attention to the six people in the middle.

I will go one step further: If what you are really seeking is a mate, not a meal ticket, not a symbol of your sexual prowess, not a status symbol, you will find him or her waiting in this pool of six. They have been there all along, but you've been ignoring them.

Am I telling you to settle? Why shouldn't you have one of your top two? I know we discussed compromise in Chapter 1, but it's so touchy and it keeps rearing its ugly little head.

There are two things to remember. The first is that you always compromise something when you form an attachment to someone else. People are so flawed and your picture is so unreasonably detailed. How come you are so willing to compromise psychological satisfaction but feel so awkward compromising your demands on sex appeal or income? It's odd, isn't it?

The second thing to remember about the top two is that they occupy this status according to social criteria *only*. They fit the picture at first glance. If you stop to consider the other six, it may turn out that you're really not compromising anything important.

Obstacles to Making the Screening Shift

I really believe strongly that this change of focus from the social to the psychological will let you maximize your chances of picking the right mate. Still, it's not always easy; there are real mental obstacles that will impede your progress. Unfortunately, the most I can do is warn you of these barriers. You will have to fight the dragons on your own.

Think it over. Wouldn't you rather have odds of eight out of ten on your side as compared with two out of ten? All you need do is shift your attitude, shift your focus, and make your happiness more important than your status.

Obstacle #1: You Can't Tell Your S's From Your P's:

You feel if you got a superstar you'd bliss out, never ask for another thing.

Yes, a rich, sexy mate can make you feel terrific—for a while. He or she *is* an achievement. You got the brass ring after a six- or seven-year merry-go-round ride through the single world. You'll celebrate your victory and you'll love yourself for being a winner.

But if all you get is Rich and Sexy, you'll still have a mountain of psychological cravings with no good way to satisfy them. You will still need someone to love you, cuddle you, talk to you, know you, play with you, laugh with you, fight with you, nurture you, plan with you, build a life with you.

If you don't pick a mate who satisfies a lot of these needs, how long do you think you're going to stay feeling so terrific? Not as long as you'd hoped. Not even as long as you thought.

At some point you grow restless, lonely, hurt, angry, lost, or disconnected. You can't understand what you two have lost. It was so much better at the beginning. You are emotionally dissatisfied. But more likely, you didn't have solid points of contact to begin with.

What to do?

You could look for someone else.

You have the choice of separating or, if you were married, of divorcing.

You have the impulse to try again with someone new, but you fear that you'll never find someone else. You worry because you know a lot of people end up choosing the wrong person twice.

You may choose to stay in the situation because:

- You feel you're too old to change.
- It's financially comfortable.
- You have children.
- You wouldn't know where to start.
- You can't bear the guilt, anger, depression, or anxiety you feel when you even think of leaving.
- You're afraid you'll never find a replacement who's as Rich and Sexy.

If you stay, you could try to find some other way to meet your psychological needs:

• You could devote yourself to your children and make them the main source of your emotional well-being. A lot of women end up here.
• You could devote yourself to your work. You are so busy, so absorbed, so invested, that you don't have time to feel lonely, or disconnected. A lot of men end up here.
• You could have an affair.
• You could develop intimate, satisfying friendships.

Each of these solutions will be partially successful. Each has its cost. An exclusive emotional investment in your children is not the best psychological environment for your child. Devotion to work is a stopgap measure. Affairs are a headache. Close friends are hard to come by.

The best way to satisfy the bulk of your emotional needs is in your relationship with your mate. Choose accordingly.

Your ability to choose accordingly will depend to a large extent on your own degree of social self-consciousness. I've argued at length for the benefits of a shift from social to psychological priorities. For most readers this will work wonders and open countless possibilities. But some of you are exquisitely sensitive to and place a great deal of emphasis on social status. You simply could not attach yourself to a woman who was not beautiful, just because she understood you, stood by you, or made you laugh. You'd feel uncomfortable married to a man with a lackluster career no matter how sexually satisfying, or loving he was. Male or female, your primary purpose in mating may not be communion or intimacy; social status may be a crucial motivation in your desire to mate at all. You may require your partner to have a high social standing in the world because you need it to increase your self-esteem, or because you find it difficult to respect people of lesser standing.

This is not an uncommon phenomenon, and it's true of all of us to some extent. Your mate is always a reflection of your social status within the group. The more uncertain you are of yourself, your power, your worth, the more important it may be for you to pick a mate who will afford you the most status. Ironically, the more elevated your own position, the more you may feel it necessary to choose a mate who is an "equal."

To the extent that you are socially self-conscious and social status is a major value for you, you must continue to be scrupulously rigid about your screening standards in column #1.

No, it's not the best reason to choose a mate, because it doesn't maximize the possibility of your having a happy, fulfilled emotional life with your chosen companion. But if that's where you are, that's where you are. Admit it, let yourself know it, and don't try to get both columns in one person. You probably won't.

Obstacle #2: The Audience Effect

When we mate we inevitably make a statement to the world about some part of who we are. It's important to all of us that the world interpret this as a positive statement.

But, as we've discussed, the world is most likely to pay attention to the social criteria, because they are the most obvious. This exerts a social pressure that makes one inclined to be more influenced by the rest of the world's opinion than by one's own. You are tempted to ignore your own feelings about someone, to be influenced more by how everyone else feels about him, than by what you feel. I think of this phenomenon as "the audience effect."

The audience effect is the sense of living your life as though other people are reviewing it, judging it, *and* you're caring a great deal about their judgment. This last part is crucial. You experience the audience effect to the extent that you really care how people judge you and need their approval or esteem.

The audience relies on social criteria. Other people are hesitant to judge whether your partner fulfills you emotionally. This hesitation is not usually motivated by tact or a notion of independence of choice. It's just too hard to see or evaluate someone's individual needs, much less how satisfying his or her mate might be. (You've been scarcely paying attention to how well someone gratifies *you* psychologically, so imagine how vague and murky that would be to someone observing the two of you.) No, around psychological satisfaction people usually adopt the pseudo-tolerant attitude, "Whatever makes you happy, dear."

Ah, but around standing in the world, society has some very definite points of view. You are marrying "well" or "beneath you," you are getting "a catch" or not.

Society here refers to your family, friends, and associates, all of whom are looking over your current prospects. They have strong attitudes about what constitutes a correct choice, and they let you know about it in a myriad of subtle and direct ways.

All of the pressure makes it difficult for you to relax your own screening criteria. You may be convinced that your own emotional needs are important, but one of these needs is often approval from the people closest to you.

You hit a roadblock. Your mother feels that the right husband for you is one who could support you. The fact that you are twenty-eight and have been supporting yourself financially for six years is irrelevant. You are drawn to creative, whimsical men who make you laugh, but whose economic prospects are shaky. You feel free to enjoy a relationship with a man like this because he makes you happy, but you can't really consider him for your mate because he doesn't fill the social criteria. Result—you remain alone. There's still no one supporting you financially and you lose out on the security of continuous psychological support as well. The only gain is in what you want to avoid: disapproval.

"Poor" is only one judgment, and one most often (and easily) applied to the choices of women. Homely, fat, short or dumb, ill-educated, rotten table manners, tacky clothes—all of these are external judgments with which you may have to cope if you shift toward pleasing yourself rather than your audience. Outrage over race, religion, family background are other obstacles with which you may have to contend.

Your family may or may not come around after you've made your choice of someone who does not meet their social standards. For example, mating outside of your race or your religion will be an issue for some families but an irredeemable catastrophe for others.

But your peers, your competition in the great social status game, will respond in a way that is largely based on your attitude and the kind of press you give your mate. It's the Beau Brummel Phenomenon. Beau Brummel occupied such elevated social standing in matters of taste in Regency England that he had only to dance with a girl and her social reputation was assured. You may be no Beau Brummel, but if you indicate that you are enjoying a happy sex life, the homeliest of choices will occupy a certain place in the fantasy life of your friends. All you have to have is the confidence that you are truly pleasing yourself and you will become an object of envy rather than criticism. It's magic.

Special Problems of Second Relationships

One group is particularly susceptible to the audience effect that pressures them to judge a mate socially: people who are divorced.

Post-divorce is such a vulnerable social state. You may feel an impulse to compare your new choices with the old one in a competitive way. Some people feel a strong desire to "outdo" their former mate.

Maybe your spouse left you for someone else. Besides everything else that costs you, the injury to your self-esteem can be severe. One of the time-honored techniques for healing wounded self-esteem is to choose a new partner who is impressive. Usually "impressive" means socially impressive.

Being left is not the only situation that can leave you vulnerable to the audience effect. Any divorce, however much of a relief it was, can leave one with a sense of failure. It is a public event, unlike an unhappy marriage that might be concealed and dealt with as a private affair. The public nature of the experience makes you particularly susceptible to the judgments of others.

Maybe you'll find it important to choose a mate who is as attractive, as tall, as stunning, as your first. Maybe you'll need one who is as successful, as important, as wealthy. The audience effect puts devastating pressure on the Rich and Sexy focus.

You may be really disconnected from your ex-spouse, but still need to "prove" to your family or friends that the divorce worked in your favor. If you were rejected, you want them to know the other person made a mistake, but you triumphed. If you were the one who left, you want to prove to your family that you did the right thing. If you remarry "better," you feel you'll convince them.

Whatever the particular circumstances of your divorce, the audience effect might motivate you to choose your second mate to prove something. I'm not saying it won't work. I'm simply suggesting that it is not the best strategy for choosing the right mate. If your new partner offers you the right relationship, and happens also to be "impressive," so much the better, but choosing "impressive" alone—without regard to what you need—is probably what got you into this situation in the first place.

Obstacle #3: The Notion of Romance

There is a fantasy bred in all of us that stands as a direct barrier to making a rational shift in your priorities for choosing a mate. It is the myth of Cosmic Romance. It is the idea that love, attraction, mating is something that happens to you, that you are helpless before its power. It is the wish that you will simply know it's right, because the fates have brought you together in an inevitable way. I touched on this myth when I discussed the phenomenon of "looking for a mate behind your own back." This fantasy can be an enormous obstacle to developing a rational plan of operation.

You may feel it is too clinical to open your options to eight out of ten candidates. You may be uncomfortable with being clear about the fact that you have selection criteria at all. You may prefer the idea that you are simply waiting for love to strike, that it will strike in its own magical fashion, and that you have no standards for a mate beyond this mystical emotional bond.

All of these feelings can make my rational approach sound like a cold shower. It's too scientific you feel, too harsh, and above all, too unromantic.

Feh, I say. And double feh. A mate is going to be the other half of your life. Don't tell me you don't have some pretty powerful assumptions about who and how you expect that person to be. If you prefer to keep yourself ignorant of those preferences, perfer the explanation of "chemistry" to self-awareness, that's entirely up to you. But I repeat, unless you know your screening principles, you won't have the opportunity to change them. And since the principles handed down to you may well not be the ones that work best today, you are leaving yourself very vulnerable.

The best thing about simply waiting for love to strike is that it is entirely out of your control. That's also the worst thing about it.

Obstacle #4: A Fixed Personal Picture

You are adamant about certain things. You've told me about them and they sound something like this: I can't get turned on by someone who is short, by a man with a beard, by a corporation type, by brunettes. I don't like Jewish men, Italian women, big women, small men, redheads, and on and on and on.

How many of these items are on your list? How much do they add to the possibilities of your being happily mated?

The fact is, when you say "I could never marry a short man," what you mean is that you don't want to—*you've decided* that a short man could never make you happy. What feels like an inviolate truth about yourself is really the expression of decisions you've made about how to choose.

It makes a big difference when you understand this distinction. If it were true that you simply, biologically, couldn't be aroused by a man with a moustache, or couldn't be happy with a tall woman, well, the whole matter would be out of your hands. It would simply be a fact of life—a limitation that you'd have to work around—but it's probably *not* true.

When you understand these as decisions, you include the option of changing them if they're criteria that don't work for you. You at least have the opportunity to examine the origin of these decisions, to judge whether you like their bases, whether they are still as appropriate to you now as they were when you made them.

You may be wondering how I can call these decisions when you don't recall making them. You've simply noted these strong preferences of yours as facts about yourself.

They are decisions nonetheless. They may have been unconscious decisions, based on positive or negative associations from your childhood. (Your Aunt May wore huge, jangly gold bracelets and she always overwhelmed you with attention. You "decide" that women decked out in jewelry aren't your type.) They may have been society's judgments to which you decided to conform. (For example, our world is maniacally harsh toward fat people and you may have decided that only a lean body could be sexually appealing to you. In another century, when society's standards of beauty were quite the opposite, so might your decision have been.) You may have made a rational, calculated judgment about the social class or religion of your mate, only to find on re-examination that the basis for your decision changed as you matured.

Whatever the nature of your decision-making process, it is important to understand that you are in control of your responses to someone's external characteristics. If you like to think of yourself as "selective" and you choose to maintain your rigid criteria, that's up to you. But you are not helpless in the face of your own screening techniques.

Obstacle #5: Rich and Sexy

I've saved this for last, because for a lot of you, it's the biggy. Even if you are an independent thinker, not especially influenced by social status or the opinions of others, you may still have difficulty abandoning category #1 as a screening priority. Rich and Sexy are very deeply ingrained.

I know that you could be tempted to redefine "rich" to mean "respectable" and "sexy" to mean "attractive, at least." In this way you could try to get around my suggestion that you abandon these outdated, biologically-derived requirements and move to more emotionally satisfying standards.

The fact remains that Rich and Sexy are nice extras, but they will not guarantee for you a psychologically satisfying bond. Here's why:

For Women Only: On Rich Men

Boy, have you been sold a bill of goods. They've told you for generations, for centuries, that you'd get to make the following kind of deal: If you promise to stay home and maintain the family, he promises to cope with the outside world for the two of you.

I only know one thing: *The deal isn't real anymore!*

It was more real for your mother, but barely. It really existed for your great-great-grandmother, but it's been fading fast ever since. The deal you thought you were making was that he'd shelter you from the outside world, while you'd create a shelter for him and your children. The key to the deal was that he'd do it for your *lifetime. Forever.*

Even a hundred years ago the deal worked. You had few opportunities to leave the home and he had little possibility of divorce.

The reality of choosing a mate in the 1980s is that the deal will work for a while. You will, if you choose, avoid the work force, tend your children, nest. Maybe you'll love it or maybe it will drive you bananas. Maybe you'll choose to live out your part of the deal because you know it's the best game in town (read *The Total Woman* by Marabel Morgan). Maybe you'll choose this deal because you're scared to death to be independent and your mate has offered you a shelter from the storm (read *The Cinderella Complex* by Colette Dowling). Maybe you got stuck with your end of the deal because men wouldn't let you have it any other way (read Betty Friedan, Germaine Greer, Marilyn French). I don't care what the reasons are, I care about one reality: The deal is temporary.

You'll live out this fantasy during your most productive work years—your twenties and thirties, perhaps into your forties, the years when adults create the basis for a satisfying work life. But for so many women, at some point, *the deal falls through.*

I didn't make this up. Consider these realities:

1. 50 percent of married women born between 1950 and 1954 will get a divorce, half within seven years of marriage.

2. Widowhood—women live almost eight years longer than men.

3. Working women—50.2 percent of married women work outside the home.

It all adds up to this: You cannot depend on a man to protect you from the economic realities of the outside world for your lifetime because, all intentions aside, he probably can't or won't.

And yet, you are still out there carrying around the image that the most desirable men are the rich ones. Rich, meaning professionally secure, materially strong. You want it because you've been taught to believe that the more he has, the better off your life will be. Even when fathers stopped asking him if he could support you, you didn't stop choosing, *above all else*, someone you thought would provide for you.

Well, some will support you, at least for a while. And then? Then you and the 2.3 kids you are responsible for are on your own. (Only 14 percent of women get awarded alimony.)

No, men are not rats, not irresponsible, not bums. It's simply that the world has changed and your illusions have not caught up with it.

You are not only likely to be economically responsible for yourself, but you *can* be. That's the other way the world shifted as the deal was falling through. Maybe you can't succeed as easily as a man can, but still and all, more and more, you can do it. That's the good news.

What does that mean for those of you who are picking a mate? It means that you are free to reorder your priorities in a more realistic fashion. When you understand that you are ultimately responsible for your own financial survival, you can put a man's financial status lower on your list.

Why look for something else that you ultimately must do for yourself, when there are so many things that you can only get from a mate? You can move professional status lower on the list of requirements and replace it with companionship, personal warmth, faithfulness, loyalty, any of the psychological requirements that can only be fulfilled by our long-term relationships.

When you have reordered your priorities you will find one outstanding fringe benefit: You are likely to make the more emotionally satisfying marriage. Do you want that or do you still want a "catch"?

For Men Only: On Sexy Women

Boy, have you been sold a bill of goods. You live in a world that has taught you to appreciate very few bodies. If you don't get to marry one of those bodies, you just don't measure up. Since hardly anyone, especially over thirty, has that body, you live with a constant underlying theme of disappointment. You wonder what you're missing. Sometimes you are driven to abandon your wife, your children, in a frenzy of trying to recoup what you are missing.

What's missing is usually that social definition of "sexy."

Sexy here means one thing—physically attractive. It refers to some constellation of anatomical parts that includes tilting breasts, curving asses, legs that look like they could wrap around your neck. It may also include a pretty face, which is preferable but not essential so long as it is not offensive. Good hair helps, though it doesn't necessarily have the impact of really tight thighs. Oh, and a relatively flat, but "sweetly curving" belly.

So, breasts, asses, legs, thighs. Sure, it sounds like a chicken dinner. Sure, lots of women have objected strenuously to your emphasis on their corporal selves. So you've done what's reasonable to do when you're under attack—you've gone underground.

You're talking meaningful relationship, but you're screening for breast size. You're talking intimacy, but you're choosing the body first, the brain an added (maybe essential) plus. You can't help it, you feel. You are, after all, a man.

Within limits, you shouldn't have to help it. A nice body in bed is a very nice experience. It's quite reasonable to prefer that you'd have this experience with your mate.

Women feel this way too. More and more they are choosing to screen for sexually attractive mates. They are beginning to develop quite explicit preferences about lean middles as opposed to spare tires, about definite musculature and narrow hips. They are talking more openly about the requirement for a matted chest and a handsome head of hair. They are looking more openly too, at nineteen-year-old lifeguards with stomachs that ripple instead of hang. Even more disconcerting, they are (very tentatively, because it is violating a great social taboo that makes you men very mad) beginning to discuss penis preference, comparing width, length, and strength.

Where does that leave you?

It leaves you where it leaves all of us, in the same foundering boat, feeling we can only be rescued at the shores of physical perfection. There is nothing wrong with having certain visual preferences. We all have aesthetic values. Other human beings who embody those values are a pleasure to look at, to fantasize about. Enjoy your fantasies, but don't let them get in your way. The problem is that while we all hold the same "high standards," most of us fail to live up to them ourselves. Yet, all of us continue to reject at first glance.

If you want to marry a body, that is your prerogative. But if you want the body and the person too, learn to enjoy a lot of different body types. Here's how a man I know put it:

"Right around the time I got pubic hair, I got a copy of *Playboy*. I think it was 1957. I was twelve.

"My images, the ones I held in my head when I jerked off, all revolved around this particular body, this sculptured fantasy. Oh a lot of different sculptures were all right but it all had to do with a certain firmness to the flesh, a sleekness about the muscles.

"One night I weakened. I won't bore you with the particulars, but a combination of "be here now" and a bottle of Pommard gave me permission to go home with an old friend who was definitely *not* my picture. I had a great time. It got me to thinking. I realized that good in bed was a lot more important to me than just looking good. It turned my sexual criteria around. Two things came out of this decision: First, I never had to deal with a possible princess who was doing me a favor just by being there. I also got laid a lot more."

How come sexual beauty is such a traditionally male screening technique? It relates directly back to our earlier discussion about male dominance. The most powerful males got the sexiest females. Likewise, having the sexiest female made you a more powerful male.

You've been looking to sexy females to provide you with that status ever since. Cavemen were scarcely looking for good communication or honesty. You *do* need both these things in a mate. How come you're still looking for the same things your ancestors were?

Because your group still values it utterly. It still gives a man enormous status to have a sexually beautiful wife. Like any of the other social standards, sexual attractiveness has its place on the list, but it probably shouldn't be first, second, and third.

I'm also recommending that you place how someone makes you feel about yourself above how someone makes you feel in bed. Keep it on the list, of course, just move it down to number three or four. It may be that how someone makes you feel in bed *is* how you feel about yourself. In that case, you have a problem that severely limits your choice of a mate.

The Gourmet Single's Guide to Screening Strangers

If you've been able to overcome, to a degree, the obstacles that we've just discussed, you are probably ready to make the shift in your screening techniques from social criteria to psychological needs.

It's a simple mental adjustment to make. You just want to loosen up your requirements on the social side, so that you can concentrate on how someone relates to you.

Naturally, you can't eliminate *all* your external standards. You just need a way to review potential candidates and eliminate only those who are *really* unacceptable to you. You need a way to screen the field.

A potential candidate is really anyone who is available, as defined by Rule #1. Realistically, though, everyone who is a potential candidate to become your mate is not acceptable to you as a real-life candidate.

Every one of you needs to be able to approach the world of possible strangers and screen out, rapidly and efficiently, all those who would not make good possibilities as your mate. You don't have the time or energy to pursue each available person to discover if he or she might be a candidate. You need a strategy to determine in the first few minutes (often seconds) whether this potential candidate could be a real candidate.

Having some useful criteria for screening is absolutely necessary. The problems begin with the criteria themselves. Unfortunately, it is not enough that your screening be rapid and efficient. It must also be reliable.

Your screening standards must reliably direct you to invest your time with people who could really become your mate. It's a pretty disappointing experience when you discover someone was a false positive—that is, he or she passed your screening but turned out to not be a very good candidate after all. False positives are disappointing but unavoidable.

What is even riskier is a false negative, that is, someone you rejected in an instant who really might have been a very successful mate. In a world where you may feel there aren't many available candidates out there, a false negative can be a disaster.

A lot of you are stuck with just this kind of unreliability in your screening strategies. You are creating a lot of false negatives. I know that you are because you are complaining that "I never meet anyone" or "There's nobody out there." That suggests to me that you are screening out a lot of possibilities.

You are also creating a lot of false positives—considering people as good candidates for mating who don't turn out that way. I know this because fifty percent of your marriages end in divorce. Fifty percent—that's a lot of false positives.

The unreliability in your screening is often due to a central problem: You are using social criteria to screen *out* instead of *in*.

Here's what happens. You have a mental picture, or a half-conscious feeling, of the sort of person who appeals to you. (In Chapter 5 we'll try to get very specific about that mental picture, so you can decide if it really works for you.) You carry that picture around as a kind of mental checklist. Maybe it includes a general age range, a certain social style, or a personality type you find especially stimulating.

Along with this mental image you've developed a set of ideas (biases/stereotypes) about how to determine if someone would match your list. *Here's the danger point.* Your assumptions had better work perfectly or you'll rule out a lot of nice people.

You walk into a party. You're a little put off to begin with because you know you *never* meet anyone at a party. Three men are at the party alone. You look them over briefly—dismiss them immediately. Why? Well, the first is wearing a leisure suit. You can barely keep a straight face. The second is short. You always envisioned yourself with a taller man. The third mentions he's an orthodontist. Just what your mother always wanted for you! Just what you always knew would bore you to death. You turn off. The next morning you report to your girlfriend, "It was so depressing—there was no one there."

You men are screening out with exactly the same capriciousness. You are at a bar. Secretly you have reservations about ever being able to take a woman seriously that you meet in a bar despite what you've read. Nevertheless, you insist to yourself that you have an open mind. Three women are standing around the room. The first offers to buy you a drink. She's somewhat attractive, but she's smoking and obviously she's "aggressive." You don't like women who might order you around. You move on. The second isn't thin enough. Forget her. The third has a good body but bad skin. While you are wavering, she mentions that she lives in the suburbs. Too much trouble. You leave.

It's interesting, isn't it, that most of our screening techniques work to screen people out, instead of in. That is, more people get screened out than are allowed in for a second glance. We are all so sure of our ability to judge, and we use it with such impunity that we often work against ourselves.

How often have you dismissed someone by saying: She's pushy. He's sloppy/wimpy. I hate his clothes. She's boring. She's a clod. He smokes. He's cheap. She's ugly. I hate glasses. I hate men in gold chains. I hate whiny women. He lives like a pig. Her friends are creepy. Those shoes turn me off. I hate capped teeth. I don't like the type. The examples could go on for pages.

What you need is a screening system that will allow you to rule people in. You need a technique that lets in the top eight and eliminates only the bottom two. You need to be able to control your tendency to judge, judge, judge. You need to order your preferences so that you can focus on eliminating those potential candidates who are really unsuitable to you, without eliminating nearly everyone else in the process.

Try the following exercise:

Imagine you are at a party, a bar, or any other social occasion where you don't know everyone. You are looking over a group of ten *available* strangers. You are screening all of them by what is immediately observable to you. (You do this all the time.) Your information is limited to what they look like, their dress, perhaps to some behavior you are able to observe, or to some conversation you overhear or participate in. Based on this information, complete this sentence:

"I wouldn't consider as a candidate for a mate anyone who _____."

1.
2.
3.

That's it. You have just set up your own screen-out rules. You're allowed three. When someone is trying to learn to view the world from a positive attitude (which is all the shift is really about), three fixed negative judgments is plenty. Of course you have an additional thirty rules lurking in your mind. We all have them. Let them go and be happy you can still hang on to three.

Think of it as being on a diet. You are, in a sense. You're putting yourself on a negative judgment diet. I know a lot of you like to binge on negative judgments, but you're on a mental health diet, for the sake of your heart.

I've worked with a number of single men and women around developing these rules. There's a lot of resistance at first. People try to get around the limit of three by being overly general, deliberately leaving themselves the option of rejecting anyone who "doesn't look right," or "seems dull," or is "obnoxious." I know it's tough to be specific. I also know that these screen-out rules can work for you.

It may be helpful to you to compare your rules with other people's.

A 26-year-old C.P.A. would not consider any woman who:

1. wore a wacked-out dress
2. was less than 4'10" or more than 5'10"
3. was scowling

Compare that with this list of a 48-year-old female advertising account executive who decided to reject any man who:

1. had no sparkle (downtrodden)—depressed
2. was slovenly—uncoordinated, shabby
3. was obese—*fat*

Here are some other examples of crucial traits that make women decide to screen men out:

1. poor hygiene habits
2. avoids eye contact
3. degrades women

Or:

1. looked dirty, sloppy
2. was bigoted
3. wore gold chains

Or:

1. looked stuffy
2. was obese or over 6'4" (as I'm only 5' tall)
3. had very poor personal hygiene—greasy hair, body odor

This woman could not hold herself to three. She added:

4. was, no, *looked*, more than twenty years older than I
5. was smoking
6. looked dissipated
7. wore polyester clothing

I know you'll want to take a look at some more of the lists
men devised to screen out women:.

1. overweight
2. bad skin
3. horrible accent

Or:

1. looked cheap (dress, jewelry)
2. was fat
3. was too young

How do you react to this one?

1. wore flat shoes
2. had small breasts
3. had short hair

Or:

1. looked masculine
2. was fat
3. was wearing really strong perfume

You can change your list of three over time, if you find
your original standards no longer hold true for you. You
must, however, limit yourself to three screen-out rules.

Three will probably seem restrictive to you, because we are
all so accustomed to enjoying long lists of things we don't
like in other people.

Actually, I feel I'm being generous. No one I've ever met
has been such an exquisite package themselves that he or she
was entitled to enjoy contempt for more than three characteristics of other human beings. It's not only self-inflating,
it's self-defeating.

Once you have your list, put it into effect. It's a bit awkward at first. Give yourself some opportunities to practice. See if it works for you. It's a simple operation, but very difficult to pull off. Make an agreement with yourself that you will allow anyone who meets Golden Rule #1—availability—to be considered by you as a candidate. The only people you are permitted to reject, utterly and without a qualm, will be those who appear to you to demonstrate one of the three items on your screen-out list. Remember, you're entitled to *three items.*

Having your strict guideline of three, and only three, will help you, if you use it scrupulously. At the very least, it will make you aware of the load of negative opinions you carry around. And *negative* opinions are still opinions—and as such, you *can* change them.

You can go beyond this awareness to an actual change, if you follow the rules strictly. To do this you actively have to follow up on relationships with people you might ordinarily reject. Talk to them. Smile across the room to someone you never would have smiled at. Invite that person for a drink.

You can do this exercise in one of two ways. You can go through the motions, or you can do it genuinely.

Going through the motions means holding on to the judgment but forcing yourself to spend time with someone. It's when you say to yourself, "Oh my God, he's wearing a toupee, yuck," and then force yourself to chat. You spend your time focusing on the toupee and his foolishness. Result: you prove you really "tried" but he's just not your type.

A genuine experience of the exercise would be to note the toupee, remember that it wasn't one of your items, and remind yourself that the toupee just isn't that important. You reinterpret it more positively, perhaps something like "he wants to look his best. He cares. Maybe he got bad advice, but it's nice of him to try." Then you chat with the person and see what else is nice about him.

It's hard to do, but it's possible. More important, it's

worthwhile. Your mate is probably hiding under a toupee, or behind glasses, being too nervous, or too loud, or too aggressive, or any of the thousand other things that are so safe to dislike.

This chapter suggests a rational shift in screening strategies that would relax the social standards you have been taught to judge by and increase the group of people who could potentially fulfill your emotional needs—security, companionship, support, and love.

In order to successfully make this shift, you need to take a hard look at yourself. Use the next chapter as a mirror.

·5·

What Makes You Bite—
What Keeps You Hooked

I 've been suggesting one thing all along: one of your problems in finding a mate is that you don't really know that much about yourself.

We all hope that "someone will come along" and don't give that much thought to the kind of choices we'll have to make when someone does. But you will have to make choices and you will need a set of priorities to guide those choices.

The first step in recognizing your priorities is to figure out how you've been picking up to this point. You need to know what makes you bite and what keeps you hooked.

Remember your wish list? (Who could forget it—it's practically a pet albatross.) The wish list in Chapter 1 was the beginning of a statement of what is important to you about a mate.

Although most of the items on that list are common to nearly everybody, a few of the points you made will begin to suggest things about you individually. For instance:

Sara's list includes "someone whose mind is a little bit 'bent'—not crazy exactly, but not conventional."

Susan insists on "someone who is mysterious, a little aloof. I don't stay interested in guys who are all over me."

Edward, reacting to a bitter divorce in the not-distant-enough past, hopes for "a woman who is content to stay home, who's not looking for a fancy social life, who will not be forever dragging me around from place to place. I want to relax!"

Rick is clear about one point: "She must be a very sexually uninhibited woman. I need someone who doesn't have a lot of rules about what's right and what's weird."

Each of these people is hinting about some trait that is central to what is attractive in other people. People are drawing the outlines of their "type."

Instant Arousal: Your Type

Knowing your "type" means knowing what you are a sucker for.

Type refers to some relatively obvious, easily discernible characteristics that immediately arouse your interest. That's type as in "I usually go for Mediterranean brunettes," or "I really turn on to jocks." Type may also be a rueful, self-mocking awareness, as when you moan, "I am hopelessly drawn to confused, struggling souls," or "All my women are a little bit crazy."

Type can refer to some alchemy of sex and status so powerful that in its presence you hear nothing but the call of your crotch, screaming "touch me, pick me, notice me." That's a phenomenon we see with the groupies of rock stars, with the women who pursue yachting men ("racer-chasers"), hockey stars ("rink rats"), with anyone driven to rub their private parts against a famous body.

It can also refer to someone who so precisely fits your mental picture of the ideal man or woman that you really resist knowing that person at all. You just want someone to be what your fantasies tell you he or she is.

Having visual or social preferences about others is perfectly natural. There are human traits and behaviors that will be immediately appealing to you. The problem comes up when you compare your real life needs in a mate with the old mental picture of your type.

Sometimes your type can stand in your way.

Many people, both male and female, confine themselves to a sexual type. ("Only tall, dark men turn me on"; "I'm a breast man and more than a handful is a must"; "I'm excited by a man who looks a little bit dirty.") A sexual type may have little or nothing in common with the sort of person who could be satisfying as a mate. Unfortunately, he who warms the genitals does not necessarily warm the heart.

Occupation and other signs of social status can also have a significant impact on your type. One woman told me that she was looking for a lawyer. Period. When I suggested that was a rather rigid approach, she thought it over again. "Okay," she relented, "he could also be a judge."

Some of you probably have read this discussion with some confusion because, you feel, you don't really have a type. Maybe your past romantic relationships have been with a wide variety of people. Perhaps you feel that you enjoy meeting people and, unless someone is really revolting to you, you'll get to know them with an open mind. If this is the case, consider yourself well ahead of the game. You've made yourself genuinely available. Still, you might want to check yourself out on this very carefully. Type is not always as conscious as it might be. The following exercise will be helpful to you, too.

Use these questions to determine your type.

Demographics

This includes all the relevant statistical information about your fantasy mate. Note aloud all of your demographic requirements. ("G.U.'s"—"Geographical Undesirables"— whether he or she lives fifty blocks or fifty miles from you— fit in here, too.)

Age
Sex
Race
Religion
Level of Education
Income Level
Occupation

Body Type
What attracts you the most readily? Reflect on height, shape (lean, long, curvy, stocky), or some specific physical feature. Are you invested in some special body parts? Are you a breast man, a leg man, an ass man? These attachments are most commonly associated with the preferences of men, but they are certainly not exclusively male.

Use the space below to list the physical traits that most attract you:

1.
2.
3.
4.
5.

Clothing
Style of dress often stirs social and sexual fantasies.

Some women are drawn to men in three-piece suits (they communicate a respectable income), or leather jackets (they suggest sexual dominance), European tailoring (they spell sophistication), jeans and crew necks (they convey a boyish *joie de vivre*), running suits and rugby shirts (they say jock, a fatal fascination for some women).

Men may be drawn to stiletto heels (they imply a garter belt, still a dominant male fetish), wrap-around skirts and sweet little blouses (they suggest high-minded attitudes and limited experience), flowing, flowered skirts and low-cut peasant blouses (they suggest fulsome earth mothers prepared to nurture).

What are your fantasy styles? List them below:

1.
2.
3.
4.
5.

Props

Props are all those appurtenances displayed publicly to deliver a message about the kind of person you are. Props may have functional value. In fact, they often do. But they are usually personalized to some degree and people read their messages.

Props include jewelry, briefcases, eye glasses, wristwatches, hats. Also automobiles, pets, home furnishings, toys.

List the props that draw you and/or ones that offend you.

1.
2.
3.
4.
5.

Personality Style

Your mental picture may not be limited to physical presence. Some personal styles of interacting in the world will have readier appeal for you than others. There may be a thousand ways to classify these superficial personality types. Some examples include: the bookish academic type, the outdoorsy type, the worldly sophisticate, the homebody, the energetic aggressive type, the "laid-back" sensitive type, the theatrical type, the shy diffident type, the corporate solid citizen, the political activist, the artistic soul, the romantic dreamer, the helpless vulnerable type. You get the idea. Of course, real people overlap categories. It's useful for you to understand the personality styles you are attracted to. If you're having difficulty with these, think back over your past relationships for more information.

List your preferred personality style below:

1.
2.
3.
4.
5.

Whether your type is something you can clearly and immediately express, or whether it remains a half-conscious set of preferences, you must still be alert to potential dangers.

Having a type can present a problem when:

- your type feels uncomfortable as your mate, or
- your potential mate isn't quite the type

Both of these can be genuine agony and both problems can be overcome if realistically choosing the right mate is your priority.

Review your answers to the exercise to see if you are setting yourself up for one of these problems. Here's how other people used them:

Fifty-two-year-old Lenny was quite explicit in this exercise. His type, he felt, could never be an appropriate wife. Lenny is fatally attracted to (and apparently attractive to) much younger women. His type is a woman in her twenties, sexy, pretty, and most of all young. He is a prominent and rather distinguished man, but he's basically very shy. He cannot resist a confident, clever twenty-two year old who is sexually aggressive and apt to do the pursuing.

The women of Lenny's generation were raised to be much more diffident about sexual pursuit. Lenny enjoys intimate friendships with several female contemporaries, but he doesn't feel especially sexually aroused. He is longing to marry and settle in, but he doesn't want to choose love at the expense of sex. His type is standing in the way.

Pam's exercise revealed a similar obstacle, though age was not the theme. She is an only child, accustomed to a great deal of affection and attention from those who love her. She is also afflicted with an only child's compulsive need to be special, to stand out in a crowd. Her exercise showed that she transferred this need to the type of men who appealed to her. She had no special preferences in demographics, body type, or clothing, but she was quite explicit about personality. Pam only feels a pull toward "high-powered men, important men. I want a man at the top—I don't care what he's at the top of. My type is the leader, the one that everyone automatically turns to for approval, for decisions. I always wanted to be his woman."

Pam could recognize the problem all too easily. These are men most accustomed to getting attention, not to giving it. She could never be more than one of the spokes in the wheel that revolves around her type of man. It's never emotionally satisfying enough for Pam.

Pam and Lenny made opposite decisions about the dilemmas presented by their type.

Lenny reviewed the problem and came to feel that the woman he would marry would need to be his type. He felt his sexuality was a central need of his, and its satisfaction was a requirement. He knew that a decision to marry a much younger woman meant a lot of social adjustments with his friends and some predictable problems a few years down the road ("When she's thirty-two, and I'm sixty-two, what then?"). But he felt he had to choose what was essential to him and let the future take care of itself.

Pam handled it differently. She realized that her high-powered lovers could never be satisfactory husbands. Pam saw that it was more important for her to feel special to someone, than for that someone to be "special" in the world.

She had one other strength—which many of you could develop—that helped her handle the problems of her type. Pam was willing to learn from experience. She had already had one brief and two long-term affairs with men who were her type. They didn't work, and the problem was always more or less the same: Pam felt neglected. She was willing to conclude from this that her type just wouldn't suit. She didn't have to keep trying it over and over, clinging to the fantasy that one of these men would be exactly her type, but different in his treatment of her. Pam still has her type. Now she uses it as the type of man to stay away from.

If you review your own exercise on type, you may be able to highlight a conflict of your own. Write yourself a note about it here.

The problem with my type is:

This problem will usually imply a choice on your part, as Lenny had to choose between sexual appeal and age appropriateness, and Pam had to choose between power and personal attention.

Write down here the needs you may have to choose between:

1.

2.

3.
4.
5.
6.

You can have a similar problem when you are involved in an ongoing serious relationship with someone, but you hold back because he or she doesn't quite fit the picture. You have a good thing going but you are reluctant to make it permanent because maybe there's someone out there who would be just as good *and* more your type.

I know this one can be tough on both parties because my husband had exactly these reservations about me. Oh, he didn't seriously doubt that he loved me, and we were a pretty good fit right from the start. But he almost wished that he wasn't so hooked because I was not the picture of the woman he always fell for.

He was a never-married thirty-five with a strong preference for very shapely women. He would describe his type as animated, athletic, and sexy. (I think of them as Sweatsuit Floozies.)

I am a short, chubby, brunette whose idea of exercise is raising my voice.

I knew the problem was serious when we went to see a rerun of *Lady and the Tramp* and he identified so strongly with the Tramp that he was depressed for a week. You know what? He got over it.

He had a choice to make—the woman who actually made him feel good about himself (me) or the type of woman he always thought would. Happily for me, he used Rule #3— and let go of his fantasy picture. Happily for him, too.

The Long-Term Pattern

Type, those relatively conscious preferences you experience, is not the only source of information necessary for you to understand how you are choosing now.

The other, trickier, area to examine, is your pattern of relationships. A pattern is a set of themes that repeat in your relationships. Though the body types, ages, and occupations of your partners may vary, there are likely to be similarities in the kinds of relationships you have. Perhaps there are similar obstacles, or similar areas of conflict, similar reluctances you experience or similar criticisms these varied people all shared about you.

The reason patterns are trickier to evaluate is that they are less obvious. They tend to be a more unconscious expression of your needs, where type is a more direct, conscious expression of preferences.

Try not to be spooked by the mysteries of the unconscious. It's nothing so magical as you may have been led to believe. The fact is that some of our motivations are less obvious, more subtle, less apparent, even to ourselves. You have to pay more attention to yourself, in a more careful way, in order to be clear about these motivations.

There's a payoff in paying this kind of attention. To some extent your pattern is less superficial and therefore more a direct expression of what is uniquely "you." Where your type is more easily influenced by the culture around you—by your social group—your pattern might be thought of as an expression of your own personal needs, a product of your own life experiences.

When I suggest you observe a pattern, I mean simply that you notice it. You don't have to ask yourself why it's there, or how you got to be this way. Just because a pattern is apparent does not mean the pattern is a problem. Those questions are really only important to answer when you want to change the pattern.

Many people who first perceive a pattern have a sort of panicky reaction. They say, "Oh my God, if that's what I'm doing, and I didn't even realize it, I'll have to *stop* doing it!"

Well, maybe you will. But it's just as likely that you won't. You see, everyone's patterns have flaws. They all reveal needs that we often wish weren't there. Needing, in and of itself, is a perfectly human state of mind.

It's okay to need companionship, love, financial support, someone to mother you, affection, laughter, shared interests, devotion, status, a family, children, a big house in the sub-urbs, travel, one home forever, the city, the country, intel-lectual stimulation, a playmate, a trouble-shooter, a sugar-daddy, someone to look up to, someone to feel better than, someone to run your home, a friend, a sex object, lust, pas-sion, someone to grow old with, someone to rescue, someone to rescue you . . .

Just as long as you don't *need them all.*

It's probably not okay to need abuse, attack, deprecation, fear, or sexual despair.

Don't fall into the pit of getting down on yourself just because you are getting a clearer picture of yourself.

Using the Exercises to Discover Your Pattern

I'm always attracted to those quizzes in ladies' magazines. You may be familiar with the type, with titles like "Your Marriage—Hot or Not," where you answer A,B,C, or D and count up the points at the end.

Don't panic when you don't see any multiple choice in the exercises in this chapter. At least you won't have to cope with the frustration of having to answer "none of the above."

These exercises are more open-ended, designed to help you draw an individual picture, instead of wedging you into a category where you don't quite fit. I think you'll find them a lot more involving and a lot more fun; kind of like the dif-ference between Go Fish and Bridge.

I can't give you a formula for mapping your unconscious choices in relationships. These patterns are often what peo-ple enter psychotherapy to discover. They get to a point where they feel they haven't been able to make a relationship work for them, but they don't know what they're doing wrong.

You may or may not be doing something wrong. What we can hope to do is to focus your attention on the fact that when you are choosing a mate, you are looking to fulfill needs that may not be all that obvious to you. I will try to point out some of the most common of these patterns. I hope it will lead you to do some productive thinking on your own.

Exercise # 1: Test Yourself Against the Rules

Name	#1 Availability	#2 No Substitutions	#3 On Emotion
1.			
2.			
3.			
4. (optional)			

In chronological order, from past to present, write the names of your three most significant past love relationships. No, you're not allowed to skip anyone you've been married to, or lived with, no matter how much you may want to forget he or she ever happened. The purpose of this exercise is to get information about your own past choices as evaluated by the three cardinal rules.

It's preferable that these relationships be over for you because time and emotional distance are great objectifiers. If you're involved with someone now and would like to examine the relationship, add him or her as a fourth name.

If you don't have three relationships to list, think for a moment why that is. It could be that you are newly divorced or widowed and your last relationship was so long-term that there simply was no one else in the picture. If that is the case, just use the relationship you had and fill in the other two names with people you've dated or thought about. If all else fails, use your parents' relationship. Understanding their patterns might give you some insight into your own.

If you can't list even one, and you're over twenty-five, you might ask yourself how available *you* are. Remember, Rule #1 goes both ways.

I am assuming that, for one reason or another, none of these relationships developed into a happy mating, or you would not be seeking a mate right now. Test the rules by applying them to these three people and see if they help you to clarify any of what went wrong in the past.

First, consider the question of availability. If there was no problem here, put an X in the box. If they were not highly available, according to the criterion described in Chapter 2, *or if you* were not available at the time, put an O in the box.

Next, consider the question of no substitutions. Could you accept them wholeheartedly, despite their limitations? If so, put an X. If you had strong reservations or were looking to make serious corrections, put an O. Try to describe the flaw ("too dumb," or "too cold," or "no ambition") so you can determine if you tend to pick people with the same limitation.

Finally, how did you feel about *yourself* with this person? If you were pleased, put an X. If you wouldn't choose to live with that overall feeling for a good, long time, put an O. Do you always feel some way about yourself in the relationship that is a problem for you ("too strong," "too responsible," "too inadequate," "too unattractive")?

Read across your chart and pay attention to the X's and O's. If you had used the three rules as guidelines, would you have chosen to invest your emotional energy and limited time in these relationships?

Try to determine if you have a pattern of violating the same rules repeatedly.

The next set of exercises involves developing one- or two-word descriptions of various aspects of a relationship.

Because many of us have difficulty labeling personality features, or subtle processes like feelings, I have included a list of descriptive adjectives that may stimulate your thinking. You might want to look over this list to see if it gives you any ideas. But don't be bound by it. Expressing something in your own words is likely to be the best way to communicate information to yourself.

- pretty, beautiful, handsome, attractive, virile, cute, sexy, *or* clumsy, awkward, homely, fat, dumpy
- intelligent, sharp, knowledgeable, quick, bright, *or* dumb, dull, dense
- exciting, spontaneous, fun, stimulating, *or* boring, dull, timid
- friendly, outgoing, pleasant, bubbly, *or* shy, isolated, diffident, mean, angry, hostile
- warm, affectionate, loving, passionate, intense, *or* cold, negative, judgmental, aloof, distant
- practical, realistic, *or* romantic, dreamy
- sophisticated, experienced, worldly, polished, *or* naive, childish, ingenuous
- selfish, egocentric, spoiled, *or* compassionate, caring, considerate
- sensitive, perceptive, intuitive, *or* rational, logical
- high-strung, anxious, nervous, tense, insecure, fearful, *or* relaxed, calm, serene, tranquil
- assertive, confrontive, aggressive, intrusive, pushy, demanding, *or* passive, wishy-washy, peace-keeper
- energetic, ambitious, driving, active, hyper, *or* lazy, slow, deliberate, satisfied
- positive, upbeat, happy, *or* sad, depressed, hopeless, negative
- devoted, direct, loyal, trustworthy, honest, sincere, *or* devious, manipulative, exploitive, insincere
- creative, original, different, impulsive, imaginative, *or* predictable, organized, compulsive

- stable, mature, *or* flaky, zany, whimsical, weird, silly, emotional, overly-sensitive, complaining, whining, temperamental
- highly verbal (talks a lot), *or* quiet
- competent, able, independent, powerful, successful, *or* inadequate, helpless, dependent, needy, jealous, possessive
- masculine, *or* feminine
- stubborn, rigid, sexist, bigoted, *or* accepting, humorous, soft, supportive, interested
- formal, neat, organized, schedules, *or* sloppy, casual, disorganized, chaotic

Exercise #2: Test Your Self-Image

Reflect again on the three names on your list. List below three adjectives that describe, in general, how these people made you feel about yourself. Complete this sentence. When I was with _____, I felt I was:

Person #1	Person #2	Person #3
1.	1.	1.
2.	2.	2.
3.	3.	3.

These adjectives don't have to all be different.

Now examine your answers. Are there any items that come up across all three relationships? Perhaps this suggests that you choose relationships that give you this sense of yourself. Perhaps part of your pattern is to seek out someone who will reinforce this part of you. Are you happy/satisfied with this?

Maybe all three lists are different. Do the differences tell you anything about the nature of the relationship?

Examine these adjectives in the chronological order that the relationships occurred. Do you see a developmental pattern? Do you see yourself seeking out new feelings about yourself? Are you happy with the shift?

Other people's lists might be helpful in understanding your own.

The first is the list of Spencer, a thirty-year-old marketing manager. He described his sense of himself within relationships to three significant women as follows:

Person #1	*Person #2*	*Person #3*
1. alive	1. warm	1. little
2. attentive	2. secure	2. insecure
3. special	3. masculine	3. jealous

All three of these relationships terminated. On reflection, Spencer said, "The problem with the first two was that I simply wasn't willing to see them through. Perhaps I wasn't ready. At the time, I felt that the women were 'too good,' 'too easy.' I guess I thought there should be more storm. Finally, I got involved with number three, the tall, thin, blue-eyed blonde of my fantasies. As you can see from my list, it was a disaster for me. But what I learned was that my first two relationships were really special. In retrospect I wish I'd married one of them. My current relationship has me right back on the positive track—but this time I appreciate it so much more. She doesn't know yet for sure, but she's the one I'm going to marry."

The second example is that of a forty-year-old divorced woman. Eileen is a very attractive, bright lady who is fighting her way through an addiction to tempestuous men.

Person #1 (a stormy college romance for three years)	*Person #2* (her husband of nine years)	*Person #3* (the man she left her husband for)
1. desirable	1. normal	1. wild

2. creative	2. competent	2. neurotic
3. romantic	3. smart	3. passionate

As her adjectives demonstrate, Eileen tends to seek out intense, stormy relationships that are usually too unstable to merit the long-term commitments of mating. She swung from this extreme to a relationship that suited her family's expectations—a "normal" professional man with whom she formed one half of the "ideal" couple for nine years. But she found the experience monotonous and dull, until she finally left in a burst of emotion attached to relationship #3.

Eileen has since ended the merry-go-round of drama that characterized her third relationship. Unfortunately, she left it for a fourth relationship that is similarly dramatic and unstable. "If only I could find a man who would combine both these sides . . ." she says wistfully. But her need for external emotional stimulation is so driving that she has a pattern of choosing her mates largely based on their ability to provide *Sturm und Drang*. The upheavals create enough emotional distance for Eileen to feel comfortably free. But they prevent her from developing the stable base she also craves.

Look at your list of adjectives. Is there a similar story of your own emotional quest, based on your adjectives, you can write?

Exercise #3: Relationship Styles
Sometimes you can discover something about yourself by examining the structural elements of a relationship. The structure refers to what happened, as opposed to the question of why it happened. You might get a clearer picture of this if you ask yourself:

	#1	#2	#3
a. How long did it last?			
b. How did you meet?			

	#1	#2	#3

c. Who ended it?

d. How much time did you spend together? What was the pattern? (lived together, dated, all week, Saturday nights)

e. Who did the pursuing—called the most, arranged future plans the most?

f. What initially attracted you?

g. What initially attracted them?

h. What did you fight about?

i. What activities took up your time together?

j. What were your complaints?

k. What were theirs?

Your goal here is to see if similar themes crop up in the outside structure of your his relationship. Do some things stay the same, only the names of the people vary?

Don noticed one thing very clearly in this exercise. Though his relationships varied in length, he always left them. And he always left with a feeling of disappointment. The pattern was the same: He was initially attracted to women who appeared to be very independent, successful in their own right. Yet in the end he felt they were too demanding, not sensitive enough to his needs.

Don had set up a paradox for himself. Though he preferred women who were self-motivated, he focused his relationships around trying to bring them under his control. He had a need to dominate strong women. Reviewing their fights, complaints, and shared activities hinted at the pattern. The women who participated in Don's own interests were "unstimulating, easily led," he complained. They didn't open enough worlds to him. But the woman who didn't participate in his interests was felt to be "selfish, uncompromising." All three of these women shared a common complaint about Don. Though they expressed it differently, the theme was the same "You're impossible." They were right. Don is not looking for a mate. He's looking for a power struggle. If he wins, he loses interest. If he is threatened with losing, he backs off.

Deborah's style exercise was confusing. Each of the relationships was quite different, ranging from a man she lived with in her twenties, through her ex-husband, and one love affair during her marriage. They each began and ended in a different way and she played different roles in each (sometimes pursuing, sometimes being courted). There was one common element. Deborah is a beauty and she felt certain that her looks were the initial attraction for each of these men. Doesn't sound like much of a problem, but it can be. Deborah relies almost entirely on her physical appearance as her coin of realm in relationships. She insists on a great deal of admiration and adulation and she doesn't expect to give much back. All of the complaints about her revolve around the theme of her defensiveness, her lack of give-and-take (Person #1 "thought I was a bitch," Person #2 "said I always wanted things my way," and Person #3 "couldn't be sure of me.") Deborah's relationships will never work out until she stops looking in the mirror.

Carole's list put the focus on a clear problem in her pattern. Carole always does the pursuing. People who pursue her, bore her. As soon as the pursuit is over, she loses interest. Either she becomes so difficult that she pushes someone away, or she leaves herself.

Check your own answers to see if there is similar information you can uncover about yourself.

The fourth area that might yield some information for you is around typical central conflicts or struggles in a relationship. When two people get together there are certain themes that are repeated. Not all of these themes will be relevant to you personally. Even for the ones that are relevant, it's interesting that across different relationships you may find a greater or lesser degree of conflict around the same problem areas.

Exercise #4: Examining the Central Themes
Below I will ask a series of questions that relate to these central themes. Review your three relationships with these questions in mind and see if you can pinpoint any areas that:

- repeatedly create problems for you
- are repeatedly sources of satisfaction for you
- can offer some explanation about what went on in that particular relationship

With respect to you and #1, #2, and #3:

1. Who was the grown-up and who was the child? If you shifted roles, around what issues were you the grown-up and when were you the child?

2. Who was the rescuer and who was the victim? That is, was one of you often the one with problems, confusion, etc., and the other one's role was to make it all right. Which of these roles do you usually assume? How satisfying is it?

3. Who was the practical one and who was the dreamer?

4. Who was the boss? Who made the rules?

5. Who was the lover and who was the beloved?

6. Within the relationship, which of you was it more important to satisfy sexually?

7. Who was the "strong" one? Who was "weaker?"

8. Who was the smart one?

9. Who was the communicator? (When there were problems, who usually precipitated their discussion?)

10. Who was the angry one? Who was the hurt one?

However you answered these questions, it's important to remember one thing: There is *no right way. There is only understanding your way.*

I mean that. It's not more correct to be the rescuer than to be the victim. It's not any "healthier" or "less neurotic" to be the grown-up than it is to be the child. In examining a pattern, the goal is not to assume that any one of these roles is more desirable than any other. The problems occur not so much because people occupy the "bad" role, but because they occupy it in a rigid way. The goal in having a pattern that works for you is to have flexibility, so that you can trade roles back and forth. Each partner should have the opportunity to be the boss, or the child, or the pursued, or the communicator.

If something comes up as a role you usually occupy across all three relationships, you may be fixed in a pattern of seeking out someone who will always play out the other half of this role. Reflect on this. Are you comfortable with it? Does it work for you? What does it cost you?

For example, I've worked with several women whose relationships reveal a pattern I've come to think of as "The Call of the Mild." These are women who repeatedly overshadow their partners in some important way.

Phyllis described this pattern in her exercise. She felt that she was most often the grown-up, the practical one. Phyllis is a 44-year-old attorney. She's sure of herself, exactly the person you'd want next to you in a crisis. In each of her relationships, her men are a little bit less sure, less focused on their goals.

Originally, Phyllis felt she needed to change this pattern. She thought it was "neurotic" of her to choose men less powerful than she.

But is it? Phyllis feels most comfortable with her life when she exercises the maximum amount of control. Her mild-mannered men allow her to do this. They really don't care that much how the books are kept or how the living room looks. They don't have to compete with Phyllis because it's not that important to them.

Phyllis needed to concentrate on the No Substitutions Rule. Maybe she resented the burden of always being responsible, but in exchange she had a partner who was willing to let her have her own way. It can be a very fair exchange.

Almost the opposite of "The Call of the Mild" is the "stable" person who is forever rescuing someone who is an emotional shipwreck.

This pattern shows up strongly in questions #2 and #7.

Bill is an extreme example of this pattern. At any given moment his current girlfriend is likely to be hospitalized for a) a mild suicide attempt or b) a toxic drug reaction or c) getting beaten up in a bar. Bill is always at hand, talking things out, taking her home, and nursing her until her next episode. She is usually helpless, tearful, confused. She has trouble being close to people. Bill is the only one she can count on. When she hits him in a fight, or goes home with one of his friends, she is always very sorry later. She has a lot of problems. Actually, so does Bill.

Exercise #5: A Summary Statement

As I said earlier, a pattern is repetitive behavior that expresses some underlying emotional need.

I know that it is often difficult to put these kinds of needs into words. Words, however, can help consolidate your thinking.

These exercises focused on your past relationships. It is easier to look at what needs were being met, than to envision the future and ask you to describe what needs you have that are yet to be met. It's easy for all of us to get caught up in how we think we should feel, rather than how we really do feel.

I know you may have changed, may have developed significantly from the person who demonstrated those patterns in the past. Nevertheless, it could be useful for you to spell out those past patterns as clearly as possible.

This exercise below organizes the information in all the previous exercises. Just look over the exercises, see what they reveal to you. Remember, you are describing what you've *done*, how you've chosen in the past. Fill in the following blanks.

I've been choosing partners who:

made me feel I was_____.
saw me as a_____kind of person.
I could expect to do_____for me.
I could offer_____to.
would feel_____toward me.
I would feel_____toward.
I think of as a_____person.

Your answers to this exercise are a summary of your past patterns in romantic relationships. It suggests that you have certain needs, follow certain scenarios. You can look for someone to fulfill these needs, or you can change these needs. But you can't ignore them.

The Bottom Line

This chapter has raised a lot of questions about how you're currently choosing a potential mate, from the people who instantly excite you through the patterns that repeatedly frustrate you.

You need to organize all of this information into some list of priorities. The priorities should help you focus on what's important to you in a relationship at this point in your life. I am going to call them your requirements. They represent the bottom line, the distilled statement of who *you* are looking for.

You may be unhappy with your current list. It may strike you as shallow, unrealistic, or crazy. Try to write it as accurately as you can—even if it offends your self-image. If you don't like something about what you need now, you can work to change it. But it doesn't work to pretend it isn't there.

To determine the bottom line, re-read your answers to the exercises. Then complete the following statement:

I know I need a mate who will:

1.
2.
3.
4.
5.

You can use this list as your personal primary assumptions about a mate. These are characteristics, circumstances, or behaviors that fill your highest priorities for a mate.

Look over your list. Does it intuitively seem correct? Does it seem to capture your feeling about what you want a mate for? If anything seems missing, add it to the list. You don't have to limit yourself to five items. Make whatever adjustments you feel are necessary. If you aren't sure what to change, leave it as is. Trust your intuition to tell you the truth.

People's lists vary widely.

A 41-year-old Main Line divorcée writes: I know I need a mate who will:

1. know how to treat and appreciate a woman
2. have status, power, and
3. money

Karen, whose case history is in the next chapter, made the following list:

1. stimulate me (mentally and physically)
2. support me
3. allow me to do 1 and 2 for him
4. be an equal partner

Mac, a college professor, has these requirements:

1. be emotionally secure
2. be steady
3. be tolerant of my eccentricities
4. be sexy
5. not be defensive

One man I spoke with really surprised himself. His list revealed that what another person would put up with in him was more important than any of her superficial characteristics. John is quite tolerant, and he requires that somebody give him the same latitude:

1. be flexible
2. be easygoing, not a complainer
3. be a little crazy, like me
4. have sense of humor

Gary is 27 years old, an engineer, and gay. He's recently ended a long-term relationship and is looking for a man who is:

1. able to make a commitment
2. stable, emotionally mature
3. fun to be with/lively
4. kind
5. shares my interests

Your list is a statement about the most important features of a mate—for you. Of course you have many other preferences about who your mate must be. Some of these preferences will loom larger than others in importance.

But your list, however long it is, represents your *requirements* in a long-term committed relationship.

You can, if you choose, learn to live with, even learn to love, a great many admittedly negative features in someone else. But you are motivated to learn this if you are very clear that someone satisfies your basic personal requirements.

Your list may be something you've known about yourself all along, or it may surprise you. Thinking clearly about your own requirements, as distinct from your family's expectations, and your friends' preferences is a difficult business. I hope these last few chapters have made that somewhat easier for you. Knowing your requirements makes it possible to please yourself.

This chapter was about taking a look at yourself. It's easiest to pick the correct mate when you have a clear idea of what you are looking for.

We've covered these possibilities:

- a pattern of violating one of the three golden rules
- a pattern of seeking relationships that help you feel a certain way about yourself

- a pattern to the structure of your relationships
- a pattern in the central themes of your relationships

You are left with one last task. Now that you have a clearer picture of your requirements in a mate, you need to learn how to identify those qualities in someone else.

·6·

Them: What's Out There

"**Y**ou'll know when it's right." Did you grow up trusting that kind of folk wisdom? Did you secretly wonder *how* you would know? Maybe you even asked. If you did, the answer was probably as vague and magical as the advice. "Don't worry, you'll just know when the time comes."

To evaluate another person you need more than simple reliance on your intuition. You need to focus your thinking, to consider realistically the evidence that's presented. And in order to think things over in a rational way, you need something to think about.

That's the purpose of this chapter. I will outline for you a series of areas that you should think seriously about as you are evaluating an on-going relationship. I cannot tell you *what to think*. But I can suggest to you *what it is important to think about*.

No Substitutions

Rule #2—No Substitutions—is your best operative rule of thumb. You will recall that No Substitutions refers to the fact that people are pretty much a package deal, bringing their difficulties along with their strengths into a relationship.

It's a common tendency to ignore problem areas when you initially become attached to someone. This is a special temptation when there are so many assets that you are just delighted to think of someone as perfect for you.

You may also be tempted to ignore the negative side when you are feeling lonely, and very anxious to find a partner. You want very much to believe you've found the right person. It may make you nervous to see this person in his or her entirety.

Some people would even present an argument against clarifying problems for themselves. They have a sense that when you focus your attention on a problem it gets bigger. One woman described this as the "naming phenomenon—once you put a label on it, it becomes real. It won't go away."

There is certainly some truth to that. Once you label something or acknowledge it directly in some other way, it does assume a sharper focus, and makes you experience it as a more permanent obstacle. The irony is, however, that whether you focus your attention on something or not, it still won't go away.

The idea that something doesn't exist when you don't notice it comes from childhood. Do you remember playing the game of peek-a-boo? You'd hide your face behind your hands and your mother would say, "Oh, where did Susie go?"

At a very early stage in our development, when you don't see something, it truly doesn't exist. It takes a while before you understand that, just because you don't see the ball, it doesn't mean there is no ball there. At around the age of six months, children develop what is called object permanence; they understand that things exist even though they don't perceive them at the moment.

We all develop object permanence very early on. Sometimes, though, little traces of this early childhood perception linger. It's easiest for them to linger around areas that make you very anxious. You may feel that it is in your best interests to deny people's liabilities as a strategy for preventing them from bothering you too much.

It's not a great strategy. Instead of these liabilities vanishing they tend to sneak up later. Then you experience a major disappointment or disillusionment: "I thought you were different . . ."; "I respected you, but now I see . . ."; "This isn't what I expected . . ."

Acknowledging limitations or problems doesn't automatically mean emphasizing them. In fact, admitting that difficulties exist is the first step toward cutting them down to size.

The problem for some of you will work in the reverse. You may be especially skilled at noting another person's weak spots. We call these kinds of people judgmental. If you are one of them you'll notice that you are usually pretty clear about the ways other people disappoint you. It just seems to jump out at you, even when you wish it didn't. Small issues may bother you way out of proportion to how much even you think they should.

You've set up quite a problem for yourself when you go about choosing a mate. When you are skilled at criticisms, it's shocking how easy flaws are to find. Your negative judgment about others will stand in the way of your ability to feel love and your ability to make a commitment. The worst risk is that you'll end up limiting your choices to those you feel are obviously "superior" to you. Then you are trapped in a relationship where you never feel quite comfortable, or secure. It's not a great formula for finding a mate.

If you feel you fit this description, you might want to review Rule #1—Availability. Often people who always find something wrong with a potential partner are people who don't really want one. They think they should want one, or a part of them wants one, but something holds them back from a genuine willingness to connect. Instead of dealing directly with this internal reservation, they go on behaving as if they are seeking a mate, but they never find someone who is "right."

If you find yourself being overly critical you will need to use the No Substitutions Rule in reverse. You will need to focus your attention on the positive in your struggle to get a clear picture of the whole person.

For example, you love her casual air, her spontaneity. She always has a new plan, an adventure under way. But it drives you berserk when she's constantly late, forgets to plan for dinner or the dry cleaners. You have to come to understand that the two go hand in hand. A talent for living sometimes precludes a knack for regularity. No Substitutions.

Whichever is your tendency, either to ignore the negatives or to overemphasize them, the goal of this chapter is to help you to form a balanced perspective of the whole person. First though, there are some technical concerns. It's one thing to consider *what* you ought to know, and quite another to figure out *when* you should know it.

The Paradox of Timing

Let's face it—it's all going to come out eventually. In an intimate relationship, where the couple spend a reasonable amount of time together on a fairly continuous basis, you'll get a pretty fair picture of the whole person.

The problem is usually that by the time you get the picture, you've already been mated for a considerable period of time. Your lives are entwined, you have joint responsibilities. If you are really dissatisfied with the whole picture as it emerges, you are pretty much stuck. You can contemplate divorce, or some other major life upheaval. You can decide to "make the best of it," which is usually a far cry from genuine acceptance.

The goal, then, is pretty obvious. You want a balanced picture of the candidate *before* you choose your mate. It will never be as full a picture, as richly detailed, as the one that develops over a long time. You cannot hope to know someone fully in advance of a life together. You wouldn't ever want to. The delights of discovery are one of the reasons two people choose to share their lives.

Your goal is to make an assessment of the major facets of someone else's personality and life circumstances. You are seeking to evaluate to what degree that person is likely to meet your needs. You've spent a fair amount of time assessing what those needs are. Now you are trying to estimate to what extent someone might satisfy those needs over a long-term relationship.

You are dealing with probabilities. There are no guarantees, of course. But you certainly can:

- make a choice that increases the likelihood of a successful relationship
- increase the likelihood of any relationship being more successful by seeing it in a realistic light

So the first goal of timing is to get a clear picture as early in the relationship as possible—certainly before you make the decision to commit yourself on a long-term basis.

This is infinitely easier to say than do. Intense emotional attachments can develop long before you have a real picture of the person. By the time you emerge from an infatuation you may already be deeply committed.

The Rule on Timing Is:

Form a mental picture of the whole person *before* you frame it and put it on your desk.

It makes sense, doesn't it? How could you make a commitment to someone before you have a picture of who he or she is?

Ah, but some of you do. You marry yourself off to a pretty face that passes you on the subway. You try your name with the last name of the new man at the office.

Those fantasies are all perfectly normal, fun, and relatively harmless. The problems develop when they significantly influence a real relationship beginning in your life.

Since you want to form this mental picture early on in your relationship, the type of beginning the relationships have will significantly influence how clear a picture you can form before your attachment becomes serious.

On Beginnings

In the countless variations on the theme of Boy-meets-Girl, one can detect certain repetitive patterns. For the sake of clarity, I'm going to describe the two extremes. Your own beginning may fall somewhere in the middle, but these extremes will alert you to the obstacles you must overcome.

Basically, there are the relationships that begin with fireworks, as compared to the ones that slowly develop over time, perhaps initially based on friendship or a common interest.

A lot of you pay lip service to the benefits of the slow-starting connections. You recognize the advantages of getting to know someone and exploring his or her character. You understand the benefits of a trust that grows gradually, of an intimacy that develops over time.

It is logical to see that the timing of information-gathering is less of a problem with this kind of beginning. You have not committed your heart. Your state of mind is open, interested. You like this person. But at the beginning you recognize quite clearly that you are not "in love." In that frame of mind you are really available to learn more about the other person. You are not so attached that you already screen out information that is unpleasant to you. You are relatively neutral, therefore relatively open to seeing the whole picture.

All this lovely logic aside, you may also be feeling disappointed. You appreciate the benefits of a slow starting rela-tionship, but you long for "passion." You are waiting for fireworks to tell you "this is it." You are wishing that you would be driven out of your mind with lust, elated by the simple smile of your partner's face. You want to fall madly in love. If you've known someone for a month and you don't feel passion, you may feel cheated.

At problem points, people whose relationships were slow starters reflect back and worry. They say, "I never felt that way about her." "We never had a passionate period." "Maybe I was never in love with him. . . ."

Our expectations are shaped to value those relationships that begin with fireworks. The net effect is that those rela-tionships that begin more quietly are undervalued. Yet those are the very ones you need to establish in order to allow yourself the time you require to develop a full picture.

If you examine the pattern, you will see how the fireworks beginning is sometimes an obstacle to developing a realistic picture.

The Ninety-Day Wonder
I've seen this pattern repeated so often. Check it out and see if you've had a similar experience.

They meet. The interest is apparent almost from the be-ginning. They are each excited by the possibilities. They be-gin to fantasize.

But these are mature adults. They don't want to rush into anything. She is particularly cautious—she's been burned be-fore. She doesn't want to get emotionally seduced again—just because he's a possibility.

But he's very interested. They really seem to click. As long as she's reserved, he's pursuing. He's comfortable in this role. He was raised to follow up with a woman who intrigued him. He's not thinking about the future, except in the most romanticized sense that this is wonderful, she's wonderful, there are no problems, and this will continue forever.

She's still cautious because she's not sure of the depth of his feeling. Her caution intrigues him, challenges him. He pursues. He calls. He wants to see her. He loves to sleep with her. They laugh over all the same things. He's there in the morning. She is reassured. He is really interested.

They are in love. They are a couple. They can't believe this miracle is happening for them. The whole world looks different. This is it.

Suddenly something shifts. She starts to believe in the future. He starts to doubt it.

What precipitates this shift? A lot of things can do it, but one or two are most common. Most often it is that somehow, somewhere, he reassures her to the point that she drops her defenses and makes a commitment. As soon as she does, he starts to back away.

The reassurances that get offered are pretty standard and perhaps inadvert. Most commonly they take one or two forms:

- he says aloud that he loves her *and/or*
- somehow the possibility of a serious future gets mentioned between them.

Either he mentions the word marriage, or the possibility of their living together, or imagines aloud their future children. He was probably fantasizing. She heard it as a signal that things are serious.

What happens? She stops holding back. She is totally there. What does he do? He gets scared and withdraws.

The instant he withdraws, she notices. She is, after all, hypersensitive to withdrawal. It may be a very subtle signal—a night he chose to be alone, a barbed remark when she had come to expect only warmth, a change in their sexual relationship, a look in the eye, a physical distance.

She notices and it makes her anxious. What does she do? Most likely—she asks him what's wrong. Most likely, he says, "Nothing—I don't know what you're talking about."

He has to deny it. For one thing, he may not have even admitted to himself that it's happening. Even if he does realize it, there's no way he can tell her about it. He cares a lot about her. He's confused. He's scared that things have gone so far. He's not sure he's ready. He's not sure she's *the one.* But he doesn't want to lose her. So he withdraws but denies it.

If she asks again—he gets angry, feels pressured. If she keeps silent—she feels anxious, insecure. The dance is on.

This entire scenario, this fireworks beginning, takes approximately ninety days, plus or minus a week.

The couple is now at the point where they can begin to work on a real relationship, struggling through the first obstacle: establishing a genuine degree of intimacy. All relationships must deal with the obstacles surrounding the development of intimacy. Some fizzle out at this point—hence the pattern of two- or three-month love affairs. Some work through this issue and develop the basis for genuine long-term commitment.

Naturally, that scenario could be played out with the sex roles reversed. She might be the pursuer, he the pursued. That's not important. What is significant is that in relationships with fireworks beginnings, both partners are more concerned with the question of forming an attachment than with the problem of realistically appraising the other. When you first meet and excite each other, you are impressed more with your idea of the other person, than with the person herself. You are attached to an image of her that attracts you. You haven't had time to get a genuine picture of the real person.

Further, your emotions work against you. You get such a strong charge from your image of this person—he seems so much like what you're looking for—that you are naturally loath to let reality burst your bubble.

When a patient comes into a session and tells me that he's fallen in love, I'm tempted to ask him to go home and come back in three months. I know that "falling in love" is a rare and beautiful state of mind and it should be enjoyed thoroughly while it lasts. Psychotherapy is a place for thoughtful scrutiny. The two are antithetical. I certainly don't want to be the one who bursts the bliss bubble. I just want to be on hand when we are back down to coping with the real world.

Don't misunderstand me. Relationships that begin with fireworks have just as much chance of working out successfully as those with a slower, saner start. It's just that the risk of maintaining the wrong ones for longer time periods is greater. If a person seems wrong for you and there was no magical beginning, you will find it easier to let go and move on. But if the initial attachment was electric, your heart may remain engaged even when reason tells you it's the wrong person.

The solution is to work on your attitude. Instead of feeling despair and disappointment when the honeymoon period ends, you might feel relief and interest. Now is when the real relationship begins. Now is when you can work on building a genuine bond. Now is when you can develop a clear picture of who the other person is. Real life really *can* be more satisfying than your fantasies, if you can make it work for you. Use the information in the rest of this chapter to help make it work.

On Living Together

Beginnings are not the only times when you can have a situation that clouds your ability to see the other person clearly. Middles can become a real problem.

I define "middle" as a point in the courtship when you act significantly to increase your overt intimacy. By overt I mean you draw your separate lives closer together in some recognizable way.

You'll stop meeting only on weekends and spend time together during the week. Perhaps you progress from making dates to simply assuming you'll be together. You may quite naturally make one of your homes the center of the relationship. Perhaps the other partner will begin to leave any necessary clothes, toiletries, books, records, in this place. You may drift into a quasi-cohabiting arrangement. Your roommate is moving out and rather than have you move to a place you can afford by yourself, your lover moves in. Anyway, you reason, you are together all the time—why should you pay two rents?

Perhaps there are no outside circumstances. You simply feel that you love each other, and you want to be together. For a variety of reasons you are not yet prepared to make a legal commitment. Living together is an easier intermediary step.

I support the idea of couples experiencing a shared home before their final commitment to each other. It's not for everyone, because many people are uncomfortable with the situation. But for people who feel at ease with this status, it can be a situation that provides a good structure for working through a lot of the issues of intimacy: power, sharing, sexual problems, money, social life.

There is, however, a high price to be paid for making this move prematurely.

Living together is a definite step on the road toward commitment. It is not a step to be taken before you've had a chance to really look clearly at the other person and see who he or she is. You will do that best when there is more distance between you.

There are a lot of problems when you do this in reverse. You may find yourself in one of those blissful beginnings where all you both want at that moment is to share a life. Something keeps you from marriage, but it's so easy to drift into being together all the time. You may want a sense of permanence and living together can satisfy that urge. So you join forces first and discover each other afterward.

The problems emerge when you are disenchanted with what you discover. Rushing into intimacy with the right person *might* be great. Rushing in with the wrong person can cost you a lot of time and pain; because, while you can rush in, it isn't so easy to rush back out.

Your lives become enmeshed. You are investing a lot of emotional energy into making it work. You don't want to lose your new home, your sense of stability. Disruption is traumatic and living together doesn't provide you with much room to back off.

You can get so caught up that the momentum of the relationship takes on a life of it's own. It pushes you forward, to more and more connection, whether you want it or not.

Living together is a time to work on the issues that couples have to come to terms with: monogamy, trust, communication, decision making, anger. You need to have a pretty clear idea that someone is likely to be the sort of person who would meet your needs before you tackle these sore spots. Living together might be something to do *after* you get a clear picture of the other person and you like what you see. It rarely provides a good atmosphere for getting that clear picture.

The paradox of timing, then, is that it takes time together really to *see* someone. But the more time you spend together, the more hooked you might get, despite what you see.

The solution is to use more care and caution in the beginning of a relationship. Go a little slower. Try to control that great leap of hope that dazzles you. You won't lose anything by controlling it. And you'll gain a lot in the long run.

At the beginning of a relationship, try consciously to evaluate it according to the three rules. If you don't have enough information to judge "no substitutions" satisfactorily, get it. Wait until the data are in before you allow yourself that burst of excitement. Don't move in first—literally or figuratively.

On Asking Questions: Styles and Strategies

So far we've been concerned with timing—when, in the course of a relationship, you should have the information available that will enable you to see the other person as a whole.

This leaves some of you with a big problem—how do you find out this sort of information? It's simple. You do these things:

* you listen
* you notice
* you ask

Listening and noticing are the less threatening of the three, although they are actually more difficult to do successfully.

People often reveal a great deal of information about themselves early in a relationship. They have a whole repertoire of favorite stories and you are a brand new audience.

The problem is that early on you may not be paying much attention to the content. Lots of things can get in the way.

For example, you might be so concerned with how someone feels about you that you aren't really paying attention to what he says about himself. Oh, you're listening hard. But you are listening for a clue as to whether he finds you attractive, whether he is responding sexually, whether he seems to like and approve of you, want you. You may be filtering everything he says for what it means about you and ignoring what it means about him.

Or you may be so caught up in those delicious, abstract conversations about Feelings or Relationships that you don't pay enough attention to what she says about her work or her mother.

It may be that early on in the relationship you weren't interested enough to listen carefully. We don't listen equally to everyone. If you're having a slow-start relationship, you may just not pay attention to the information presented in the early conversations.

Good listening can also be a problem when you don't like what you hear. One way to handle bothersome information is simply not to hear it. For example, you hear quickly that he is divorced, but it takes a while to hear that he phones his ex twice a week. You may hear that she loves to cook, but miss the information that her weight is a serious struggle.

Listening involves paying attention to what is not said as well as what is. It means hearing the gaps in the information as well as the information itself. That's a fairly sophisticated job of listening and a hard one to carry off when you are emotionally involved with the person who is talking.

Listening, however well you develop the skill, will rarely be enough to give you all the information you need. We all screen our presentations to others with some degree of care. We want to make a positive impression. We may hint at the warts but we rarely expose them directly.

Besides, to know someone fully you must know not only where they are, but how they arrived there. You need a background, a sense of her history. In the significant areas where your conversations have not already yielded up the information, you will need to inquire.

For some of you this will be no problem. You are quite comfortable setting out directly to discover what you are interested in knowing. You ask, you pay attention to the answers, and if you don't get what you're looking for, you ask again.

In fact, you might be so comfortable with this technique that you are tempted to overdo. You can easily be experienced as intrusive by someone who is more sensitive to issues of privacy than you are. The best strategy for you is to pay as much attention to how comfortable the other person is in responding, as you do to what his response is. Try to back off some if your inquiries seem to stir up a lot of tension. The fact that the topic makes someone so uncomfortable has a lot of information for you in and of itself.

Asking people questions, particularly about themselves, is a sensitive process. I hear men complain about it frequently. They often feel that women are interviewing them immediately, rather than simply getting to know them.

Carl, a 28-year-old single engineer, put it this way. "What I really resent is when a woman asks me 'What do you do?' in the first three minutes. I went to a singles' club dinner party last week. Both women seated with me rushed to find out what I did for a living. It was about the third question— right after my first and last name. I felt like they might as well ask me how much I make. I would never ask a strange woman for that kind of information."

No Carl, you probably wouldn't. But not because men are less crass than women, or women are innately more intrusive than men. It's just that both you and the women at that dinner party were screening potential candidates. Your screening for Sexy does not require that you ask any questions. You get to look her over, judge her face and body, and make your decision.

Her screening for Rich unfortunately requires some information from you. She doesn't want to judge you just by your appearance. She knows from experience that some extraordinarily scruffy men hold decent, respectable jobs. She has to ask.

But Carl is right about one thing. There are ways and ways of asking. Just as a woman may be offended by a man who crudely and obviously looks her over, a man is justified in being offput by someone who is obviously assessing his social status and income potential.

I am advising that both men and women need certain data about a potential mate in order to make a reasonable selection. But you don't need the old standard data on how much of a "catch" this person might be in the first fifteen minutes.

At the first meeting, don't ask for much personal history. Wait to see what emerges in the conversation. If someone alludes to his work, it's perfectly okay to ask him to tell you more. But so often we come off sounding like we are interviewing a job applicant!

On the second meeting, you might give someone an open-ended question like "I really don't know much about you. Tell me about yourself." This gives your partner a chance to choose the information he'd like to share.

As time goes on, if you are listening carefully, a great deal of background will be filled in. You may eventually realize that there are areas where you don't have a clear enough picture. This is the time to ask directly. By this time, you should have some sort of connection with the person that makes discussing private issues less threatening.

I cannot give you an exact time frame for the gathering of this data. Roughly, I'd suggest that within two months you'll want at least the outlines of most of the important areas of information. As we go through the different areas where you will want to gather data, I'll give you some points on appropriate timing.

Taking a Case History

When a physician evaluates a new patient, he or she takes a medical case history, collecting all sorts of physical information that may or may not be related to the current problem. It's important to have a whole portrait of a person's physical development in order to make a thorough evaluation.

When a psychologist evaluates a new patient, it's also useful to develop a picture of the person's past history. We are concerned not simply with working on the problem that brings someone in, but with understanding how the problem developed, what areas of life it is impinging upon, and where the strengths lie.

I suggest you learn to make a similar case history profile of a potential mate. Your goal is to develop a rounded picture of a person so that you can identify strengths and problem areas you might experience as a couple.

Here is a detailed outline:

Demographics

You will surely find this the easiest information to gather. It is the sort of information that should emerge in the first few dates. This should be obvious, but you'd be amazed at the number of people who just ignore these parameters of another person's life. They include:

Age—Sex—Race—Religion
Level of Education
Marital Status
Number of Dependents
Place of Residence

Functioning in the World

We begin with these because they are easier for you to objectify. When you get the knack of evaluating this level of functioning, you can move on to the really important areas of functioning in a relationship.

Vocational Functioning

This is a work history that you might actually get in part from someone's résumé. (You don't actually have to ask for a résumé. Just don't ignore it if it floats under your nose.) You will want a clear idea of where someone is in his career development, what his current job is, and what he actually does there—not just the title but the quality and content of his or her day. Also:

- You will want a sense of his or her job performance, both currently and in former positions. How did earlier jobs end? What did the candidate's bosses think of her? What kind of worker is he?

- How much time does the current job take up? What is the life rhythm around this job? i.e. 9 to 5; highly demanding—maybe 50 to 60 hours a week; erratic, flexible schedule, sometimes very busy, sometimes free to play; involved a lot/some travel. There are external circumstances that will very much shape the pattern of your life together. It helps to look at it objectively. For many people, especially those who have invested in their work/life (which includes most men and some women), work is like a template laid over the week. Anyplace the holes happen to fall is the room available for a relationship. It helps a lot if the holes on the candidate's template fall in a similar pattern to your own.

- It's interesting to know someone's career aspirations, although I hesitate to focus your attention here because this tends to be so overemphasized anyway. Often we fall in love less with the person someone is, than with the person someone is planning to be. This is one of the great difficulties of marrying young. One or both partners may still be training for their careers. They have not experienced the setbacks, failures, or obstacles that tend to occur later in one's career development. One idealizes the goal—"S/He'll be a lawyer, a doctor, an architect, run the family business, raise the kids"—because there's less experience with the realities of living the goal and with the obstacles that can interfere with it. Training is a stage where your goal is to earn the credentials that allow you to enter the field. Once you are beyond training, your job is to become a "success" in the field, however you define that. This is considerably more difficult.

- You might want to know if you will be either invited or expected to participate in the current or future jobs. (She was a dreamy-eyed poet. He is a corporate vice-president.

Now she's writing a monthly newsletter full of promotions, transfers, and detailed explanations of retirement benefits. How did it happen?) Participation can be anything from active problem solving or contributing to getting the job itself done, doing support tasks from clerical work, or bookkeeping to professional socializing. The key words here are "invited or expected."

Financial Functioning
You will have to draw your own conclusions as to the importance of *how much* money the candidate makes. I don't think it's very important, but you may feel it is. If it's crucial, find out.

In any case, though, you should take a careful look at what someone *does* with the money he or she makes.

- How many dependents are there?
- Is there debt? To what degree? You will, after all, marry these debts.
- How does he or she handle money? What is the balance between saving and spending money? In that range between "nothing but the best" and "I love to get a great bargain," where would you put his or her financial philosophy?
- What is his or her financial history? Has he or she ever experienced very wealthy periods or very deprived times? How did he or she cope with these? This information is treated by most people as highly confidential. You may not know the amount of debt someone owes though you've known him or her for years. Before you marry you must have a realistic picture of your partner's financial obligations. While you will need to tread lightly here because it's a sensitive subject, as your relationship becomes more serious you should open up the topic. Traditionally male relatives used to provide this service for innocent females. We are all on our own now, and no one, male or female, can afford that

much innocence. The earlier in a relationship you know about it, the easier it will be to make peace with.

The other information related to financial functioning is often available if you pay attention. People are handling money all around you. You might want to discuss some of these things with the candidate. Share your attitudes about money. Be careful though. In conversations of this kind it is hard just to listen. People have strong feelings about money. When someone has a different attitude, we tend to think of it as "wrong." When you think someone is "wrong," you may be tempted to convince that person of what is "right."

The purpose of this conversation is not to negotiate your financial differences. It is simply to open the door for sharing your current financial thinking. So, keep your purpose in mind—say "uh-huh" a lot and don't get hooked into an argument.

Social History

People's patterns of social relationships shift a lot through various phases of life. Single people tend to have a stronger network of intimate friends who fill some of the psychological needs later met by a mate. You do want some idea of how the candidate tends to connect with other people. You might want to look at:

• Whether this person tends to have a wide range of acquaintances, or a few close friends.
• Is he or she most comfortable in groups or one-to-one?
• If possible, you'd like to know his or her socializing pattern. Does this person like to spend a fair amount of time alone? Does he or she like to stick close to home or to go out a lot? Does he or she like to spend a lot of time around others?

Don't get sidetracked around whether you like his or her friends. If they are really horrible, criminal, or addicted, you might legitimately begin to wonder. But, if they just aren't your type, I wouldn't worry about it. There are many factors like jealousy or cliquishness that make it hard to connect with the friends of your new relationship. Time often takes care of these problems.

To some degree, the fact that the two of you are a new couple will disrupt each of your normal patterns of socializing. Observation then will yield less information in this area. You'll have to ask.

Ethical/Moral Stance

It's pretty pat to say that people benefit from sharing the same value system. It's easy to screen out someone whose beliefs offend you. But the gray areas can be a problem.

We are often drawn to people whose ethical stance is different from our own. People who feel guilty or inhibited about "being shrewd" or "cutting corners" are often drawn to those who pride themselves on these skills. There is a feeling that "I'm not sharp enough when I deal with the world. I'm glad my partner can take care of that." Or you may find yourself drawn to someone who is a "better person" than you are. You admire his or her ethical attitude and feel it could improve you.

I would remind you of one problem. When we appraise someone's ethics we tend to think of them as rules for behaviors they use to deal with the outside world. They are. But they are also the rules for behavior they will use within your relationship.

If someone is a shrewd negotiator in the office, he or she will be equally shrewd when you are arguing over your next vacation. If he cheats on his expense account and his taxes, doesn't pay his debts, exploits his employees, etc., well, you know what you can expect. Likewise, someone who has a fairly rigid moral code and feels strongly about what is right or wrong, is letting you know what is expected of you.

Political and Religious Views

If politics is not an investment for you, you may not be interested. But if you feel strongly one way or the other, you will want to get a clear sense of the candidate's views on the matter.

Religion is a similar issue. For those of you who are relatively indifferent, this will be less important. But if one partner feels deeply about this, there usually are expectations about the other's participation.

Some couples successfully agree to differ on issues of politics and religion. If you have significant differences, this is a good strategy. If you can't agree to differ, it can create some very sore spots.

Range of Interests

Under this category you might include:

- skills
- hobbies
- leisure activities

You are interested in these for two reasons. Obviously, it would be nice if you shared some of these, because then each of you would have a playmate. You will also want to note to what degree you will be expected or invited to participate.

I don't think the degree to which you share these interests is as important as noting to what degree someone has outside interests. Interests represent the degree to which someone is connected to the outside world. It is some measure of the life spark, of energy level. The content of interests may shift over time, but the degree to which someone was active in the outside world in the past is telling.

As a rule of thumb, the degree to which people are active in the outside world is the degree to which they will be able independently to fulfill some of their psychological needs when they have mated. Conversely, people who are not very involved with ongoing projects, hobbies, regular pastimes, are likely to depend on you more to fill this gap. There are pros and cons to both. Think over which suits you the best.

This is an area where you can feel quite a bit more comfortable asking. It's good conversational focus early in a relationship because people get to tell you about things they like and don't expect you to judge them for it.

Drug and Alcohol Habits

- what are they now/what is the history
- can you share them
- can you live with them

Observe. If you suspect there's a behavior that's a problem for you, ask. If you have evidence that abuse might be a problem, multiply the candidate's answer by at least two. People who abuse drugs or alcohol tend to minimize their reports.

This kind of information should give you a pretty complete picture of someone's level of functioning in the outside world. Keeping that same objective frame of mind, you want to try to evaluate the candidate's functioning in a relationship.

Functioning in a Relationship

Patterns from the Past

Just as you learned about your own patterns by using three relationships from the past, so you can look most clearly at someone else by evaluating his track record.

It's true that your source of information is biased. You will probably get to hear only one side of the relationship. Several students have asked if they should try to interview an ex-spouse. I would find it difficult to get beyond the awkwardness of such a conversation.

When you evaluate someone's functioning in a relationship you are essentially looking to clarify his pattern. You'd like to know:

- How long these relationships lasted?
- How did they end?
- Who left?
- What kind of complaints does the candidate have about a former partner? Listen very carefully to these. You are very likely to hear the same complaints about yourself. If he thought his ex was childish, you are likely to hear him accuse you of immaturity. If her former lover left her alone at parties, you'll have to stick like glue to convince her you're not the same kind of flirt.
- What kind of partners were chosen in the past? Do you know his or her type?
- How was money handled in these relationships?
- What was the pattern of sexual activity? Who initiated it? Were there any sexual problems? How were these handled? Touchy, touchy. You are *not* (Don't, definitely don't) trying to find out which of you was better in bed (even if you're dying to know). You really can only benefit from knowing how your partner worked through a sexual problem in the past, and where the sensitive areas might be.
- What was the candidate's typical role in these relationships. Was it the rescuer/victim; pursuer/pursued; communicator/non-verbal one; grown-up/kid; boss/follower?

Family Patterns

Your family is the place where you first learn how to be in a close relationship with another person. Understanding someone's family pattern will give you some insight into what someone might have to offer to your relationship.

• What is his or her title in the family? i.e. the smart one, the pretty one, the creative one, the problem person, the oversensitive one, the black sheep, the favorite, the baby, the misfit, etc.?
• How does the family show affection?
• How does the family fight?
• What are a husband's duties and responsibilities in this family? What are the wife's?
• It's interesting to note someone's current relationship with other family members—how attached/dependent on his parents he is, how she feels about her parents, what he is angry with his parents over, what her parents expect of her.

Internal Functioning

What we've collected so far is largely data about how someone behaves in the world, and with other people. There is another, internal dimension that strongly influences your understanding of what someone might offer you in a relationship. This is the information about someone's internal thoughts, feelings, and concerns. Some of these will surface later to have major impact on your relationship. For example:

• It isn't enough to know someone's job, you must also have a picture of the degree of job satisfaction. Job dissatisfaction suggests the possibility of impending change.
• What are his or her aspirations, vision of the future?
• How concrete are his or her plans for arriving at that future?
• What is he or she afraid of?
• What does someone appreciate most about himself or herself? What is most bothersome?

• How does he or she handle anger? Is he or she a yeller, a sulker, the sort who gets depressed when angry ("You hurt me . . ."); the sort who gets depressed when someone is angry with him; the passive type (anything you want, honey . . .); the confrontive type; one of those people who leaves the room in the middle of a fight; someone who holds a grudge; someone who explodes easily; someone who holds it all in, but looks angry; someone who gets over it fast; someone who carries anger for several hours, or several days; someone who gets physically ill?

When the person is angry with you does he or she punish you by:

1. withholding sex
2. withholding verbal communication (the silent treatment)
3. withholding physical contact
4. withholding basic nurturing (cooking your meal, bringing you medicine, mixing your drink)
5. leaving you (withholding everything)

• What makes him anxious? How does she handle her anxiety? Does she kick the dog, withdraw, get depressed, overeat, drink more, increase her drug intake, get physically ill, become a baby, talk it out, turn to friends, turn to you, talk faster, cry?

You'll notice that the lists of behaviors for handling both anxiety and anger sound kind of awful. Actually, the experiences of being angry yourself, being the object of someone's anger, or being anxious are pretty awful in themselves. None of the ways we handle them is too attractive. It's true that some are more mature than others, and some will work better for you than others. Whatever your candidate's style of handling anger or anxiety, it's preferable that his or her style be one by which you are neither utterly intimidated nor utterly tormented.

You get this kind of information by observing how the candidate typically reacts to these feelings when the situations come up. If you've never experienced the person when he or she is angry or anxious, you don't know him or her well enough yet.

- What is she hoping to find in a mate? What are his primary needs in a relationship?
- What does he or she appreciate most about you? What are their internal reservations about you? What conflicts are they struggling with as they move toward considering a commitment to you?

Personality

Most of the major features we include in personality have been covered indirectly in all of the preceding categories. I only want to draw your attention to a few special areas we may have overlooked:

- Sense of humor.

A lot of you list this as a top requirement for a mate. I'd certainly agree. I would warn you, though, to be clear about your definition. Sense of humor may mean the ability to tell a good story. To me it means the ability to see the humorous side of life—especially the ability to laugh at life—and even more, the ability to laugh at yourself. Everyone likes to see him- or herself like this. Take a closer look. If you are someone who takes yourself very seriously, you will have difficulty laughing at yourself. You'll probably do best with a like-minded mate. A person with a lively sense of the ridiculous will be constantly hurting your feelings.

- Organizational style.

Life is one long janitorial job. Not everybody cleans up his act in the same way. You're not looking for a perfect match—you're looking for a style you can tolerate. You know the things I'm talking about—how does he or she pay bills, do dishes, clean clothes, return phone calls, keep appointments, etc.

• Temperament.

Temperament refers to someone's internal constitution. I think of it as a kind of emotional thermometer, measuring the intensity of someone's emotional reaction to the world. It's here that we use descriptions like "hot-headed," "cold," "restrained," "warm," "exhuberant," "emotional," "low-key." You should be able to describe your picture of the candidate's overall temperament. Later, in the exercise section, you'll be able to reflect on what aspects of this temperament might be a problem for you.

Case History Exercise

If you'd like to try out the case history method, here's a good way to go about it. Pick one of your long-term relationships. It can be one that's on-going, or one of the three that you've been using so far in this book.

You will need paper and two colored pens. I used red and green. Write "A Case History of_____" at the top of the page, and proceed to write down all the information you have, using the categories in this chapter as a guide.

Remember these categories include:

I. Demographic Data
II. Functioning in the World
   A. Vocational Functioning
   B. Financial
   C. Social History
   D. Ethical/Moral Stance
   E. Political/Religious Views

    F. Range of Interests
    G. Drug & Alcohol Habits
III. Functioning in a Relationship
    A. Pattern of Past Relationships
    B. Family Patterns
    C. Functioning Within Themselves
    D. Personality Characteristics

Review these categories as I've elaborated them in this chapter to help detail your answers in each of these areas. It may take a while, but it could be worth it for you.

It's a lot, isn't it? Don't be overwhelmed by it. A great deal of this information is already floating around in your head. I've only suggested a structure for organizing it.

Still, you won't know all the answers. What's interesting is to discover how much you do know and where the gaps are. It's a structure to help you realize what areas you haven't explored, and how you feel about what you do know.

Once you've written out a case history, here's how to use it: Go back over the items and *circle in red any areas* that could be problems for you. I emphasize "problems for you." You aren't trying to point out their problems. You are trying to identify qualities or situations of theirs that might be difficult for you to accept.

For example, he might have a problem controlling his smoking, but it's not a problem for you because you smoke even more. Or maybe she has problems with her mother, but her mother lives three thousand miles away so it's really not a problem with which you must deal. On the other hand, he might enjoy screaming and yelling, while you find it abusive and miserable. That's your problem. She might happily spend her income on lots of clothes and vacations, while you feel money is meant to be saved for the future. You have a problem.

So, review the case history and circle in red all of the areas of information that are troublesome to you in one way or another. These areas in red point to most of the issues you will have to accept, negotiate, alter, or adapt to in order fully to live up to the rule, No Substitutions.

Next, circle in green all those areas where you believe your information is incomplete. The amount of green showing is some measure of your degree of intimacy—the more green, the less you really know him.

Intimacy is not just spending time with someone or working out a relationship with him, it's really coming to know someone else. All of the areas where you've circled green indicate gaps in the development of your intimacy. Naturally, there will be plenty of gaps. It takes such a long time to *really* know someone. It's the reward of a long-term relationship.

What is interesting to note is the specific areas where you lack information. The areas where you don't know the answers are the issues that you've chosen to ignore and/or about which he hasn't been very forthcoming. Pay attention to which areas these are. That may tell you something.

Maybe Karen's case history will be helpful to you. At the time she wrote this, she was involved in a year-long, though irregular, relationship with Marco. Karen is twenty-nine now, an unusually capable office manager whose lifelong curse has been obesity. Naturally, her relationships with men have been colored by her weight, though the exact connection has never been completely clear to her. At the beginning of her relationship with Marco, she was embarking on an extended diet with the goal of losing seventy pounds. Her diet was very absorbing and did help to keep the relationship in some perspective. However, when Marco withdrew for a period of two months or so, early in their courtship, saying things were "too serious" and he "couldn't handle it," it threw her. She regained some weight, went into a brief depression, and generally withdrew.

Finally, she pulled herself together and reestablished her diet. Shortly thereafter Marco reappeared. They began dating again, though on an infrequent basis—once every week to ten days. Marco had some family crisis that kept him tied up at home. Karen described the relationship as "very serious," and indeed the two had discussed marriage on several occasions ("When we're married . . ."; "If we were married . . .").

Here's the case history she wrote:

Marco—Case History
Demographics:
    40 Male—White—Catholic
    Divorced—ex-wife—problematic personality
    One Dependent—what about future?
Work History:
    Self-Employed
    Hard working, very ambitious
    Left previous employer to open own business
    Flexible work schedule (mostly)
Career aspirations:
    To own business properties that will provide enough
        income to take more time off (just about there)
    Will be "invited" to participate in decision making:
        "expected" to be supportive of business decisions
Money:
    Very well off
    No significant debts
    Spending pattern is practical in business
    Free with relaxation expenses (dinners, vacation, gifts)
    Responsible with money
    Has experienced hard times—built up business into
        what it is now
Social History:
    Few close friends, a lot of acquaintances

One-to-one (most comfortable in)
Fair amount of time alone
Don't know very many of his friends
Ethical/Moral:
  Shrewd in business
Political/Religious Views:
  Not important
Range of Interests:
  Carpentry
  Business activities
  Reading
  Avid movie buff
  Dancing
Drug/Alcohol:
  No problem
Patterns from the Past:
  Former marriage: seven years
  Ended: Divorced
  He left, but was her choice
Complaints of Former wife:
  Spoiled, never satisfied, not affectionate, miserable
Money handled:
  He earned, she spent
Sexual Activity:
  He initiated; she withdrew after child born
Role:
  Provider, pursuer, grown-up
Family Patterns:
  Title: smart one; responsible; decision-maker; favorite
  Don't know how family fights—brothers yell
  Husband's duties: Provider, "strong"
  Very attached to family—not dependent—they are
    more dependent on him
  Good relationship with one brother—not with other (is
    demanding)

Acts as parent to parents
Functioning Within Themselves:
> Very happy and satisfied with career—loves work
> Aspirations to become even more successful
> Concrete plans
> Afraid of failure (business and social)
> Appreciates his success (self-made, self-starter)
> Anger, usually talks it out; sometimes quiet

Anxiety:
> Sometimes talks
> Sometimes withdraws—disappears (once)

Hoping to find in a mate:
> Companion, someone to share *all* aspects of life, lover,
> Nurturing person

Appreciates in me:
> Intelligence
> Sense of Humor
> Take-care type
> Similar values
> Family-Oriented

Reservations:
> Weight
> Fear of me because I represent a serious relationship

Here's what Karen circled in red as potential problems:

• Divorced with one child. She noted that his ex-wife had some sort of "problem-personality," but she wasn't sure how troublesome it would be. She was also concerned because, though he left, the divorce seemed to be his ex-wife's decision. Where did this leave Marco?

• Handling anxiety—Marco sometimes withdraws/disappears when he's anxious. He's done it to her once—will it happen again?

• His family (parents, brothers and sister) is very dependent on him. He complains that one brother is "demanding." It's the same complaint he had about his wife. What does "demanding" mean?

- Her weight was a problem for him. Basically she sympathized, but sometimes she worried about what would happen if she didn't keep up the good work.

None of these concerns seemed radically to challenge Karen's requirements that her mate would:

1. stimulate her
2. support her
3. allow her to do #1 and #2 for him
4. be an equal partner

She had some reservations on #3 (How much stimulation did she provide him if he worried about her body? And how much support could she give him if he always took everything on his own shoulders?) On balance, however, the picture was positive.

Karen circled in green the areas she felt she didn't have sufficient information about. These included:

- how people in his family fight
- who his friends are; how he relates to them
- what his "type" really is
- how things ended with his wife

Though she didn't know enough about his response to the divorce, she felt reasonably reassured. If they could work out the problems of this withdrawing, they could probably make a wonderful match. She loved and respected him, their values were very similar. Karen recognized that marrying Marco meant assuming the important role of wife-of-eldest-son in a highly entwined Italian clan. She welcomed it.

Seven months after Karen wrote her case history, I phoned her for permission to use it in this book. She willingly agreed, adding only, "I wish I could add a few things now." Seems she and Marco had parted ways some six weeks earlier. After he brought her home to meet his mother and look at the apartment he was buying where they'd probably live, things got a little strained. Marco kept telling Karen that he had too many demands from his family to spend more time with her now. He repeatedly invited her to break up if she wasn't satisfied with things as they were. One evening, surprising even herself, she took him up on his invitation. She hasn't heard from him since.

In retrospect, she had included all the data in her case history, but she hadn't recognized its significance. Marco was really right for her, but not ready for her. He was constantly inviting her to become "too demanding" so he could back off. The more weight she lost, the more appropriate for him she became and the more burdened and anxious he felt. Marco was not available.

Evaluating the Data

The case history provides you with the data. Now you, like Karen, need a way to think about what the information means.

When you complete an objective appraisal of another person, there will always be liabilities as well as assets. It's easy to leap to the conclusion that you are best off choosing a mate where the positives outweigh the negatives.

It won't work. We are not yet mere computer banks. A simple estimation of the pluses and minuses won't yield you any useful information.

The question is not how many liabilities someone has, but which ones. You can afford to compromise, tolerate, or otherwise adjust to anyone's negative features, as long as these do not fall into the area of your primary assumptions.

Recall your list of primary assumptions from the end of Chapter 4. Rewrite them here. I know I need a mate who will:

1.
2.
3.
4.
5.

Now, match these with the areas you have circled in red. Do any of the areas circled in red suggest problems with the candidate's meeting one of your requirements?

For example, perhaps item two on your list is "be faithful to me." In the three months you've known this person, you feel he has been faithful to you. But when you pay attention to his pattern in past relationships you note that the candidate has a history of cheating on his partner. That's an area you'd have circled in red. You would have to acknowledge that at some point in the relationship, you'll have to live with that kind of problem. It's not a certainty, mind you. Yes, people do change, but it isn't wise to count on it. It's wiser to acknowledge the probability and decide if you could handle it. Could you relax the requirements for the sake of all the other pluses this person is offering you? Could you find a way to cope that would handle the situation should it arise?

If the answer is no—"I couldn't tolerate it," "I couldn't live with it"—that outweighs a whole slew of pluses. Your requirements must be met or dropped.

Let's face it. At the beginning of a relationship there is so much hope, so much fantasy, that this sort of objective view is tough. We pretend a lot to ourselves. We cross our mental fingers and ignore the data in front of our noses. We just want *someone* so much.

Perhaps you are only concerned right now with finding

someone. The kicker is that right on the heels of finding someone, comes the struggle called Making It Work. Fantasy is a big help in finding someone, but it is a real obstacle to Making It Work. You will have to decide how important it is to you that it works. If that's very important to you, you'll need to take your requirements very seriously as well.

Beyond your personal requirements there are some common problems people confront when they evaluate a case history.

How Do You Evaluate a Bad Track Record?

She's been divorced twice and had just broken up with a man she was living with when you met her. She's thirty-three, and she's dynamite both to look at and to be with. Best of all, she loves you, she talks to you, and she listens to you. She's seriously attached to you. But you're uneasy about her string of failures.

You're right to be concerned. But there's no reason to be hopeless.

Pay close attention to her pattern in past relationships. If you don't have enough information about the pattern, get it. Then try to determine whether your own relationship with her mirrors her pattern, or whether there has been a shift. Ask yourself what is similar about you and her former choices. Does she play a similar role in all of these relationships, including yours? Were they good relationships, despite the divorces. (Divorce is not necessarily the signal of a bad relationship? It's a signal that something ended. Good things end too.)

If you feel that your relationship really represents a shift in her pattern, perhaps a maturational step, you could feel more comfortable about it. You would have reason to take a bet on it.

If the similarities between your relationship and her past relationships are really strong, hesitate. You are choosing to go around the same old track, with someone who has a bad track record.

How Do You Evaluate a Significant Status Difference?

"I love him, and he meets all of my requirements, plus some of my preferences—as long as we're alone. But I really feel uncomfortable about his background. I'm an associate professor and he never graduated from high school. It's not that even—he's smart enough in his own way.

"But he's a construction worker, and I just can't picture myself living that kind of life. Maybe he could fit into mine—but I don't see it. He doesn't really fit in with my friends. They seem to treat him differently, or maybe we both just imagine it. But he's not really comfortable either. I do love him, I think. I haven't met anyone in a long time who I feel this way about. But I wonder if I could ever really be happy being his wife."

Social status differences are a serious consideration. They create a big problem, for women especially. We have a marrying principle in our society that is called Female Hypergamy. This means that men are permitted to marry "down" (the Prince and the Showgirl myth) while women aspire to marry "up." This works out pretty well as long as you have a lot of men at the top socially, and a lot of women at the bottom.

The problem this presents is that the women at the "top"—by virtue of their educational level, family of origin, professional status, or income level—have no where to go. They seek to marry equals, or better. But the number of available men up there is severely diminished. It's the same problem for men at the "bottom." They seek to marry on their level or down, but there is no down.

This process makes one thing inevitable. Many people will have to look outside their expected social class to find a mate.

Looking outside your social class can work well if you are willing to let go of your prejudices and come to respect someone whose social class you may have looked down on.

The problem in these kinds of matings is that the person from the "superior" class, whether male or female, often expects a reward for their superiority. There is sometimes a theme in these couplings where one partner is communicating to another, "I married you . . . I'm more than you deserve . . . You owe me."

They are not alone in propagating this fantasy. Often their partner really does feel inferior, intimidated. They can be thrilled to have been chosen and really do have a sense of "owing something." They agree that in this relationship it is only right to be "one-down." They are grateful to be in it at all.

You are certainly welcome to marry into this kind of relationship, if it fills your own basic requirements. But be warned of one pitfall: You can't expect anyone to be grateful forever.

How Do You Evaluate Sexual Problems, Especially Early in a Relationship?

"Boy, it's really terrific, except in bed. We worked together for quite a while before anything romantic really started. Well, maybe it was always in the back of my mind, I don't know. Anyway, I think he's so cute and we get along incredibly. He says he's fallen in love with me. Maybe I have too, fallen in love with him, I mean. But there's a problem. He can't get it up. I mean, he's impotent. It really doesn't bother me so much—maybe it's a little frustrating, but not as much as you'd think. He feels just awful about it. It's not all the time, but it's a lot. He says maybe he's just scared of getting involved—that I'm the first person he's cared about since he left Donna. I don't know what to think."

This is a problem that comes up (or doesn't, more to the

point) a lot. Of course, it doesn't have to be impotence. Sexual problems between otherwise compatible couples can include premature ejaculation, difficulty with orgasm, painful intercourse, sexual inhibitions, etc.

Remember, we're talking about a situation where both partners find each other sexually attractive. It's just that when they actually get down to it, there's something that isn't working right.

Usually, these problems come up more with slow-start relationships, where the couple has had some time to develop an attachment before they discovered their sexual problem. One night stands with strangers that don't work sexually are unlikely to be pursued. But romantic thunderbolts can also inspire a desire to work things out.

Here's my best advice on how to evaluate the situation: Don't devote yourself to curing someone else's sex problem unless you:

- seriously consider them a mate, or
- are a licensed sex therapist, or
- understand that you are doing it because it really is better to give than to receive.

In other words, don't attempt to cure the sexual problems of someone you don't consider your potential mate. In other less intimate situations, sexual problems can be catching.

By catching, I am not referring to those trivial or tragic diseases that God dealt us in the same hand with sex—just to balance things out. I am referring specifically to the psychological aches that come from sharing the sexual problems of a casual lover. Other people's sexual problems lead us to worry about our own sexuality. Is he impotent because he's anxious or because I'm intimidating? Is she unresponsive because she's inhibited or because I'm clumsy?

In an important relationship when these fears come up,

you get to work them through. This means you talk, you worry, you agonize, you experiment, you talk some more, you talk to yourself, you seek professional help, and, like as not, it gets better. It's difficult, and it hurts. It's worth it. This is a lot to go through for someone else's problem, unless that someone is very important to you.

I'm sure you're right at the Catch-22 by now. You are asking how you are supposed to know at an early stage whether this is worth working out. I don't think that's as much a problem as it seems. It's not the answer to that question that's so difficult, it's struggling to raise the question itself.

Some of you prefer to think of every new romantic relationship as important, at the beginning. It gives you hope. That's fine. If, early in this important relationship, sexual problems are a big issue, stop and take a more careful look than you might ordinarily. If the overall situation seems compatible or possibly compatible with the three golden rules, go for it. Working it out may be worthwhile. Don't let problem sex scare you off. But if the situation is clearly in violation of one of the rules, someone else is going to benefit from all your sexual patience. That is simply an act of generosity. Make sure that's what you have in mind.

What Changes/What Doesn't

In the end of any evaluation there is the big question: How do you know what's going to change, and what you can expect to live with forever?

No one, and no profession, can accurately predict change in human behavior. What the science of human behavior can do is to try to understand the factors that make change more or less probable. I'm giving myself an out. I can't predict change with perfect certainty any more than anyone else. But I can offer some advice based on experience.

Traditionally, the easiest areas to change are matters of taste and life-style. Oddly enough, an extraordinary number of you reject out of hand perfectly nice people whose clothes are a turnoff. Yet lots of people are amenable to a guiding hand in their wardrobe. Not everyone, of course—but enough so that rejecting potential candidates who are poorly dressed is rash.

Likewise, all those areas that reflect taste, including furnishings, props, cultural appreciation, etc., can be expected to mature. If these are areas of particular concern for you, you can expect to exercise your influence in a direction that suits you.

Not everything is so easily influenced.

When you are evaluating the liabilities circled red in your case history:

Don't

- expect to cure an alcoholic
- expect to clean up someone's drug problem
- try to "cure" a homosexual
- try to make someone lose weight
- try to make someone quit smoking
- expect someone whom you think of as a "slob" to ever be what you think of as "neat"
- expect to rescue a crazy person
- expect fidelity where none was previously demonstrated
- expect to cure a football addict
- expect to keep someone on the straight and narrow
- expect someone to stay the same
- expect someone to be what you expect

You cannot change someone. But you can support someone who is trying to change himself. Your participation can make the difference in whether your partner changes or not. You can join them at the AA meeting; you can exercise with your struggling chubbette; you can turn your smoker onto aerobic exercise; you can teach a messy mind how to organize a file, if he or she wants to learn. You can support the people you love, make it easier for them to do what they want to do; your help can make the difference between their success and failure. You can help them do what they want to do, but you can't make them do it.

The last two chapters have given you the tools you need for understanding yourself and developing a pretty shrewd picture of someone else. There's one last thing you need to make these tools work for you. It's time for a final attitude check.

·7·

Attitude Is Everything

T he most important factor in successfully choosing a mate is summed up in the title of this chapter. You can incorporate all of the principles in this book and make them work for you or you can find them useless. The key to the difference will be in your attitude.

Good attitude is the ability to appreciate the positive. The secret to finding a mate is being willing to find one. Being willing means having a positive attitude toward your candidates. It means:

- being willing to love a real person
- with all the flaws
- as long as he or she meets most of your basic needs for psychological security
  companionship
  intimacy
- and, most of your basic biologically derived needs for sexual satisfaction and economic compatibility

You are quite right to insist on a mate satisfying each of these needs to some extent.

Your obstacles are centered around the very narrow range of people you've come to believe could meet these needs. You've gotten stuck on a negative attitude that functions to rule out a lot more people than it rules in.

You've spent a lot of time deciding that you don't like a lot of things. You don't like people who crowd you and you don't like too much distance. You don't like them older or younger or short or fat or poor or brash, or dumb, or weak, or whatever else is on your list of rules. You carry around with you a thousand negative judgments and you limit your choices to the few people who pass your screening.

A positive attitude has a lot fewer rules. It enjoys a thousand facets of human behavior, so that nearly everyone it encounters offers something to enjoy. From this huge selection of pleasures, the positive attitude selects its mate from the ones who offer the most satisfaction.

Let's take an example. Remember the romantic concept that there is one "right person" for everyone and all you have to do is find each other. There's a certain appeal to this kind of thinking. It elevates love as a magical, special, once-in-a-lifetime event. We all have to react to this point of view. I know it was a problem for me—I can get very sappy. The idea of one magical person had a strong pull. It also made me nervous. I knew that if there really was one right person, with my luck the one with my name on him would be wandering around in Hong Kong or Tuvalu. So I decided to believe that there were thousands of possibilities.

In general, I advise that whenever you have to choose between two beliefs for which you have no factual evidence—like, Is there really a God? or Is there really only one person for me?—choose the belief that works to most improve your experience of life.

You Could Believe:

Only one or possibly a small few, of the people you meet could make you happy by being your mate.

Consequence of Belief:

You try to figure out what this person would be like, so you'll know him when you run into him. You decide the age, race, sex, physical appearance, character, sense of humor, value system, politics, sexual performance, life-style, and on and on. Then, you carry these assumptions and preferences around with you and proceed to rule out nearly everyone who doesn't fit this picture. Naturally, you rule them out, and quickly too. You don't want to "waste time." You are, after all, only looking for your one person.

Or You Could Believe:

That there are so many people with so many different things to offer, many of them could make you happy in a lot of different ways.

Consequence of Belief:

You don't develop a lot of rules about how potential mates should be. You simply enjoy a lot of the ways that they are. You don't know which relationships will develop into something more. But you appreciate so many different things about people that you are open to connecting with a great many of them. In other words, you are willing. You have a positive attitude.

Positive attitude is not mere wishful thinking. It is not a matter of keeping your fingers crossed and hoping for the best. Positive attitude is the ability to perceive things in their best light. It is, above all, a willingness to let things be good.

Once you can see the enormous benefits of assuming a positive attitude, you may be motivated to move your own attitude in that direction. In order to allow a more positive attitude to develop, you will be forced to work past some internal obstacles.

What gets in the way of positive attitude?

Obstacle #1: Believing in Criticism

Many of you regulate yourself by self-criticism. You call yourself fat, hoping it will motivate you to diet. You belittle your accomplishments in an effort to drive yourself harder. You make every effort to be aware of your failings on the theory that this will motivate you to improve.

To a certain extent, it works. To an even larger extent, it costs you. It costs you the experience of pleasure, pride, self-satisfaction. It costs you because it interferes with loving yourself.

The same kind of rationale can interfere with your loving a mate.

It is astonishing to me how driven people are to point out flaws or problems. There's a rationale behind it that goes something like this: "If I look pleased with this person, they won't try harder. They'll think I'm satisfied and they'll quit improving. I've got to keep after them."

Parents often adopt this peculiar stance in a misguided effort toward helping a child develop. You come home with a report card full of B's and your parents feel obliged to remind you that they aren't A's. You manage the softball team and you get the message that the honor society would also be nice. They do it to each other too. Mom gives a dinner party and Dad points out that it was all great except the hors d'oeuvres. Dad gets a raise and Mom says she hopes the next one won't be such a long time coming.

The thinking behind this is that if you love someone you should help that person to improve—which is all right as far as it goes. But the behavior that follows from this thinking is a real drag. It is negative, unrewarding, critical, and unloving (and it usually doesn't work).

The effect that behavior has on you, if you are the one doling it out, is even worse. In order to maintain motivation, you have to focus on the negative. You constantly have to be aware of the ways in which you are being disappointed. You have to cling to the negative, to focus on it.

Criticism in and of itself is not an effective strategy for changing someone's behavior. Even when it does work, you hardly know it. You remain focused on what's missing and you can't afford to enjoy what's there.

Obstacle #2: Your Sense of Superiority

The willingness to see things in their best light usually means sacrificing some of your sense of superiority.

You'll notice that people who feel superior, whether in taste, intelligence, social class, or style, usually establish their position through maximizing their dissatisfactions. They make a lot of negative judgments about other people, things, clothes, food, props, behaviors, an endless stream of issues about which they decide to feel displeased, dissatisfied, or critical.

Often these are people who pride themselves on their high standards or their "pickiness." It's as if the choosier one is, the more elite one feels. For them, a willingness to see things positively is a willingness to compromise, to lower one's standards.

Isn't it silly? What could possibly be good about having standards that are difficult to meet, or being the sort of person who is difficult to please? If you are difficult to please, you will, by definition, not be pleased very often. You are set up to experience most things and most people as a disappointment, as less than you hope for or need. Superiority maximizes your chances for feeling bad about something and minimizes your chances to feel good about something. Why would people want to run their lives stacking the odds against themselves?

I don't mean to be ingenuous. I understand that being critical is one way of increasing your self-worth. If you can increase your sense of superiority by disdaining many other people, you can feel pretty important in your own eyes. But you do it at the cost of the pleasure you experience in life.

You also, ironically, do it at the cost of your own stable self-esteem. As I said earlier, people who pride themselves on being "choosy" are often drawn to others whom they perceive as superior, even to themselves. Then they are cast into a painful sense of inferiority, of competition, that interferes with their ability to have a mature relationship between equals.

A positive attitude, the willingness to perceive things in their best light, is the best basis for genuine self-esteem. As you learn to experience a lot more facets of the world in a positive light, so you will learn to experience more facets of yourself positively.

Often patients who are commenting critically about possible partners, defend themselves thusly: "I know I'm hard on other people, but I'm even harder on myself." That's usually true. People with "high standards" are often ruthlessly self-critical. This defense is presented as if to say, "I'm entitled to judge others harshly. After all, I'm fair. I'm just as hard on myself."

This neat little self-defeating package serves only to create more and more negative judgments. The harder you are on yourself, the harder you feel you are entitled to be toward others. The harder you are on others, the more you feel you should tighten up on yourself and so it cycles on.

Obstacle #3: Negativity as Leverage

Some of you feel most powerful when you are saying no. You feel that to tolerate another person's liabilities is to weaken and give in.

Having a sense of power in a relationship is crucial. It goes beyond needing to feel superior. Even people who basically accept each other and love each other will need to experience a sense of their own power to influence events, to determine decisions.

Having critical reservations can be one strategy for establishing that power. This strategy works by communicating "I love you, but . . ." The "but" represents a withholding on your part. It's a way to keep your distance, to encourage courting. It suggests that the other person should make compromises in order to counteract that "but." It can be a very powerful position.

It can also cost you more than you gain. To maintain the stance "I love you, but . . ." you have to abandon your positive attitude. You have to remind yourself of the negative and keep it sharply focused in your mind. When you keep the negatives front and center you cut into your own experience of pleasure. What you gain in the experience of power, you lose in the experience of loving. I think you lose more than you gain.

There are so many other ways to establish power in a relationship, beside the strategy of withholding. You can have your complaints attended to much more efficiently when you shift from "I love you, but . . ." to "I love you, and . . ."

Obstacle #4: Your Sense of Being Entitled

In order to develop the most useful attitude toward choosing a mate, you will need to rid yourself of the sense of being "entitled."

Entitled implies that what someone does for you, or brings to you, is no more nor less than you deserve. It is the quickest road to losing both appreciation and the ability to see things in the best light.

Entitled is how a man might feel when he comes home to find dinner cooked and ready. Instead of appreciation, he often accepts it as his due. After all, he worked all day, isn't he entitled to have dinner waiting? He may even turn this gift into a negative experience because it wasn't the dinner he wanted, or it wasn't served when he wanted it.

Entitled is how many women feel about having someone else earn the money for the bills. Instead of appreciating it, she often expects it. After all, she is running the house, caring for the children. She can't be two places at once. She may even turn this gift into a negative experience because it isn't enough money, or the job deprives her of companionship.

The truth is that lots of men work all day and come home to fix their own dinners. Lots of women are in the unenviable position of caring for a home, children, and earning the income as well. Anyone who has someone to help them with these parts of life is not getting what they are entitled to, they are getting a gift.

Young couples often have particular difficulty in this area. Because they lack the experience to teach them otherwise, they develop expectations of a mate based on reruns of Ozzie and Harriet. To the extent that someone fulfills this picture, he or she is merely doing what is expected. It's perceived as nothing special and therefore less appreciated. But let someone violate the picture and there is a sense of deep disappointment or outrage. There is a feeling of not getting what a wife or a husband is "entitled" to get.

Positive attitude means appreciating what's offered rather than noting what is absent. Once you've decided you can make peace with the No Substitutions Rule, you simply let go of your reservations and focus your attention on the positive part of the deal.

There's no way you can feel "entitled" to anything someone gives you and still draw the benefits of a positive attitude. Once you feel someone owes you something, everything you get will be simple payment of the debt. All you'll notice is where he or she didn't pay up.

Developing Your Positive Attitude

A positive attitude will serve you in every area of your life. We are concerned here with your willingness to choose a mate, but many of the same strategies will apply across the board.

Strategy #1: Practice Saying "It's Not a Problem"

Practice this phrase: "It's not a problem." This phrase is the byword of the most positive, energetic woman I know. She's a woman who handles the logistics of a large family, a large corporation, and the social demands of a huge number of people who crave her company. No matter what conflicts arise, no matter what crises befall her, her first response is generally, "Don't worry, it's not a problem."

As soon as she takes the stance, people around her are soothed and encouraged. They are mobilized to cope, to be flexible. She cares about her own needs and she cares about other people's feelings. Her attitude has a way of minimizing the obstacles that arise when she is trying to satisfy both sides.

Of course the obstacles are still there. But her attitude reduces them, making others feel they are surmountable. Once people believe that something can be worked out, it's amazing how creative they can become at generating solutions.

It's a great phrase to incorporate into your repertoire.

Force yourself to use it two or three times a day, until it becomes spontaneous. It will have a powerful effect on your own ability to solve problems and on the attitude of people around you.

The payoff between you and your potential mate will be significant. It will help you both to be more flexible as you work out the normal difficulties of any relationship.

Strategy #2: Learn to Pick Your Issues

When you are burdened with a lot of negative judgments, lots of problems and disappointments arise. One way to discipline yourself in a positive direction is to learn to pick your issues and then really dismiss the others. For example, you are considering as your mate a woman who talks too much in the morning, gets loud when she drinks, and spends money irresponsibly. Positive attitude can handle the first two: She can handle the first by cooking breakfast in the morning and leaving you in peace. ("It's not a problem. I'll just go do breakfast. I like to be active in the morning.") Maybe you'll handle her loudness by deciding to let go of some of your own social inhibitions. ("It's not a problem. I'm only worrying about what other people think. I've decided to stop caring.")

These plans and attitude shifts can get rid of the small stuff so that when a real value conflict comes up, you have room to deal with it. You are able to focus and say, "I have a problem with the way you handle money. Let's try to solve it." What you've done is to pick your issue.

Every single annoying area does not have to be handled as a major upheaval. Most can be readily resolved by a flexible positive attitude on both your parts. Some issues will involve real conflicts, compromise, and sacrifice. You want to be able to separate these from what are only minor adjustments for the sake of harmony. If you don't make this kind of distinction, you end up doing what marital therapists refer to as "the kitchen sink."

"The kitchen sink" is a description of the following kind of a behavior during a fight: You begin by discussing the money problem, but instead of your doing some creative problem solving, you use the time to tell each other how angry you are that there *is* a problem. Pretty soon you are hauling out all your old angers about past problems, about how you hate her drinking and how she bothers you in the morning. You are, in short, throwing in "everything but the kitchen sink."

It's a very unproductive way to solve a problem.

A positive attitude requires that you pick as your issues those that are really important to you, that present real problems every time they arise. And then you let go of the rest.

Do not allow yourself to raise every single adjustment or compromise as an issue.

Strategy #3: Give Up Your Internal Accounting System

So often we are unable to let go of the list of adjustments and compromises we make for the sake of a relationship. We have an internal accounting system that is constantly figuring who-did-what-for-whom. Unfortunately, this accounting system tends to weigh everything together. It also tends to be very biased in the direction of recording more of what you gave than what you got. It is naturally skewed in the direction of making sure that you aren't cheated. And while you are paying so much attention to not being cheated, you miss much of what you are getting.

The balance in your account is not the important issue. As long as your basic needs are met, you can devote yourself to giving. You can't lose.

A Powerful Attitude

Positive attitude is one half of *attitude is everything.*

The other half is Powerful Attitude. Powerful attitude has nothing to do with power over another person. It means having power over yourself.

It is not especially difficult, and therefore not especially impressive to have a good deal of power over other people.

Inherit your father's business and presto! you have power over all the employees. Threaten to commit suicide and *voilà!* you have the power to make a lot of other people feel anxious or guilty or trapped.

You can fight to have power over other people or you can fall into it. It's an interesting situation to be in and a lot of people aspire to it.

What is considerably more difficult, but commensurately more interesting, is to have power over yourself. Power means being as thoughtful as possible about where your own interests lie. It means being able to differentiate what you want and need from what others expect you to want and need. Power refers to your willingness to get yourself to act in your own interests, despite the many lures in your path. It includes the ability to examine your own thoughts and feelings with some degree of dispassion. Finally, it means you have the drive to develop personally, to mature in your thinking, to give up the illusions and rescue fantasies you once depended on. Power over yourself is the power not just to face reality, but to fall in love with it.

You certainly cannot control all your thoughts and feelings. But surely you believe that you can influence some of them on your own behalf. If it made your life richer to enjoy more people, certainly you'd work to limit the critical barriers you erect to keep people away.

In choosing a mate, Powerful Attitude is one that says: I can change. I can find a mate who is right for me. I can readjust my criteria to include more people who may be right for me. I can stop prejudging the world and begin enjoying it. I am willing to be surprised.

Yes, But . . .

I am imagining your response to this kind of attitude as you are reading it: "Yes, but . . ."

That's "Yes, but . . ." as in "Yes, but I can't help how I feel." "Yes, but that's the way I am." "Yes, a positive attitude would be nice, but I've been conditioned to expect certain things." "Yes, but most people just don't appeal to me."

There is one universal "Yes, but . . ." that is the biggest obstacle to choosing the right mate.

"Yes, but . . . I just don't meet that many people who 'turn me on.'"

Here is the best example of dead-end thinking. You may agree with the logic of everything else in this book but allow yourself to get absolutely stuck in the face of your initial physiological response.

"Turn me on" implies the most passive way of connecting with someone. It suggests that all you need to do is stand in front of someone and magic or chemistry has to do the rest.

I repeat, you are welcome to await chemistry. Just remember, unless you own DuPont ("Better Living Through Chemistry") it's not a profitable wait.

Okay, so you're not that interested in or attracted to that many other people. That is entirely your decision. Don't confuse your deciding not to be interested or attracted, with the truth about whether they are really interesting or attractive.

Many people confuse their attitudes with the truth. That man seems weak to me, therefore he is weak. She seems dull to me, therefore she is dull. We confuse our reaction to people with truths about people

If you perceive something as the truth about someone else, you are powerless to change it. Only they can change it. But if you understand that your perception of others has more to do with what is true about you than what is true about them, you have the power to alter your attitude to suit you.

A man may be 5'5". That's what is true about him. When you look at him and decide he's "too short," that judgment says something that's true about you, that is, that *you* think 5'5" is too short. You can't change his height. But any time you want to change your judgment you are free to do so.

Getting "turned on" to someone is also a decision. It just doesn't feel like one to you.

You've taken a whole lot of rules about desirable mates and/or desirable sexual partners and digested them thoroughly. Then you've used these rules to program your body to respond accordingly.

You can relax the rules or rewrite them completely whenever you choose. All you will need is a Powerful Attitude.

You see, there is really a huge range of people who are sexually attractive. No, I don't include everyone because it isn't practical. I'll stick with the same eight-out-of-ten-goal we developed in the rational model. Eight out of ten available strangers are potential mates.

You could probably develop a sexual appreciation for eight out of ten of the available candidates you meet. Someone will, you know. Why should that person get the kick and not you?

Partly you've learned to restrict the people who "turn you on" because the rules are pretty strict about who you are allowed to act on those feelings with. They have to be a particular sex, race, age, marital status, before society feels it's okay to Do It. If you Do It with the wrong person, you often get into big trouble. One strategy for staying out of trouble is to simply restrict the number of people you want to Do It with. Just don't get turned on very often.

It's a pretty overcautious step.

We make a smaller and smaller circle of people to whom we can respond sexually. When you get in the habit of controlling your sexual arousal in this fashion, you limit yourself to those candidates whose sexual appeal is so initially powerful that it overwhelms your inhibitions. You don't have to limit yourself this way to stay out of trouble.

Feeling sexually aroused is not the same as acting on it. Feeling is not acting. You can enjoy the feelings of your own sexual response to someone in a private way. You may choose to act on these feelings where the actions are comfortable and productive for you. Or, you may have the opposite problem: "Yes, but I don't get turned on when I wish I would. Perfectly appropriate people leave me cold. I want all the wrong ones."

The problem is not that all the wrong people get an easy rise out of you. It's that not enough of the right people do. Of course, some people will have a more immediate sexual or emotional impact on you.

Yes, it's important to feel a sexual pull toward a candidate. And yes, you will feel this pull more easily, more readily, with some few people.

But don't limit yourself to those few, just because you have to do so little work to feel the pull. Most likely they are the easiest to respond to because they have some quality that you've been conditioned to react to. Just because it's easier to respond to them doesn't mean they are the only "natural" or "true" responses.

The most sexually comfortable people are those who have easy access to their own sexual arousal. They don't suppress it when they experience these feelings for someone "inappropriate." They don't create a narrow group of people who passively "turn them on." They are comfortable turning on to a whole range of people. They enjoy feeling sexually aroused and they indulge in this feeling as often as possible.

It's a radical idea. It means you could come to enjoy your sexuality, enjoy your sexual responses to others, and enjoy their sexual appreciation of you. You could enjoy it with more people, more often, and not get into any trouble, because feeling sexually aroused is not necessarily deciding to act. With this kind of payoff, why not try for it?

The first step toward freeing up your sexual response is to decide to do it. You must give up your investment in being "picky" or "difficult to please." That's easy to do once you realize that the main result of being difficult to turn on is that you feel turned on less often. What's good about that?

Second, you must give up the belief that you have no control over your sexual responses. It is pointless to argue the "truth" of that belief. What is important is the consequences of the belief. If you believe you have no control, you will do nothing but wait to see how you react to someone. If you believe you have some or a great deal of control, you'll begin to use that control to your own advantage.

Why not try it?

If you decide that you can see the benefits of responding sexually to a greater number of people, you may want to try the following exercises. They are all designed to make you more aware of yourself sexually and to broaden the range of other people whom you "turn on to."

1. Take a few of the people you "don't think of that way" and deliberately think of them sexually. People you experience in the most neuter fashion are not neuter to someone else. Although their sexuality, and their sexual appeal, may not be obvious to you—it's there. If you deliberately draw your attention to it, it will increase your possibility of responding to it.

Have a positive sexual fantasy about someone you wouldn't ordinarily think of "that way." Imagine them making love, imagine them naked. Find a body part that appeals to you and focus on it to the exclusion of everything else. You can find something sexually attractive about nearly everyone. All you have to do is allow that sexually attractive part to turn you on.

2. Notice other people's sexuality more. Watch someone caressing a drink or fondling a cigarette. Watch how someone touches himself or another during a conversation. Crotch watch.

3. Play a game of making someone aware of your physical self. Consciously lean forward, cross your legs, bite a string off his jacket, drink from her glass, stare at his lips, imagine kissing her. When someone becomes aware of you physically, it's often a turn on.

4. Force yourself to notice someone's sexual response to you. Simply fantasize one, if it isn't obvious. Say to yourself, "He's thinking of touching my breasts." "She's thinking of undressing me." One of the best ways to turn on to more people, is to allow yourself to enjoy the number of people that turn on to you.

The goal of all of this is to be less affected by your own conditioned sexual responses. The more people you feel sexual toward, the more fun it is. And, the more people you have to choose from.

The solution to your "Yes, but . . ." is this: Learn to turn yourself on. Learn to experience your sexual arousal toward more and more people. It's private, it's free, it's fun, and it's possible.

From that pool, choose the partner who satisfies your need for intimacy, for companionship, for security, for love. You will be choosing the right person to build your life with.

This is a Powerful Attitude. It suggests that all your thoughts, judgments, and attitudes are open to your own review. You may have picked some up along the way from your family, your friends, your reading, your general observation of things. Just as you picked them up, you are free to discard any that get in the way. You control your own standards. Make them work for you.

You'll know if an attitude or judgment isn't working for you when it:

- decreases your chances for experiencing pleasure
- limits the range of people you can feel comfortable with
- restricts the kind of experiences you are open to

Here, in a nutshell, you have the best strategy for choosing a mate:

1. Widen your pool of candidates.
2. Be clear about what you really require.
3. Only require what you must. Insist on that, relax about the rest.
4. Take a very hard look at the other person. Let yourself see what's there.

A positive attitude toward others and a powerful attitude toward yourself are the final, necessary elements to correctly choosing a mate. If you develop them, you'll be one step ahead. Because these two factors—a willingness to see others positively, and a willingness to curb your own negativity—are also the two best strategies, once you've chosen a mate, for making it work.

You have all the tools you need now for choosing the right mate. You know what you want, you know how to figure out what they've got, and you're in the frame of mind to make it all work for you.

Unfortunately, you won't be able to find the absolutely #1 best candidate. I already married him.

Index